handy homework helper

Geography

Writers:
Susan Bloom
Maggie Ronzani

Consultant:
Phil Klein, Ph.D.

Publications International, Ltd.

Susan Bloom is a freelance writer and editor with Creative Services Associates, Inc., a publisher of educational materials for over 15 years. She has taught composition and literature at a community college for 15 years. She holds a B.S. in English from Southern Methodist University and an M.A. in English from the University of California-Los Angeles.

Maggie Ronzani is a writer and editor with Creative Services Associates, Inc., a publisher of educational materials for over 15 years. She has over 25 years experience in educational publishing. She has an A.B. in English from Creighton University in Omaha and an M.B.A. in Marketing from DePaul University in Chicago.

Phil Klein, Ph.D., is a Geography Education Specialist for Encyclopedia Britannica Educational Corporation. He has written numerous publications including *Geographic Inquiry into Global Issues, Europe and the World in Geography Education,* and the *Journal of Geography.* His teaching experience includes geography education at both the precollegiate and college levels. He is a member of the Association of American Geographers and the National Council for Geographic Education.

Photo Research: Joyce Stirniman/Creative Services Associates, Inc.

Cover photography: Siede Preis Photography

Models and agencies: McBlaine & Associates, Inc.: Tony Torres; **Royal Modeling Management:** Roger Kung, LaTanya M. Burton-Love, Stephanie Meyer, Mark Elliot Thostesen.

Photo credits: Bettmann Archive: 64, 93, 98 (bottom), 101 (bottom); **Corbis:** 29 (top right), 107 (bottom); **FPG International:** 44; Gary Buss: 29 (bottom); Charles Fitch: 102; Kenneth Garrett: 63 (top left); Greg Gilman: 30 (top); Jeri Gleiter: 75; Peter Gridley: 27 (bottom); Richard Harrington: 108; Michael Hart: 34 (bottom); S. Kanno: 31 (bottom); Alan Kearney: 27 (top); Ed Taylor Studio: 72 (bottom left); T. Tracy: 72 (bottom right); Travelpix: 29 (top left), 48 (top); **Globe Photos, Inc.:** 19 (bottom); **International Stock:** Roberto Arakaki: 69 (top); Warren Faidley: 120 (top); Bob Firth: 120 (bottom); Michele & Tom Grimm: 52 (top); Andre Jenny: 35 (top); Buddy Mays: 19 (top); Mark Newman: 115 (top); Stockman: 11 (bottom); Johnny Stockshooter: 58; Vision Impact: contents (bottom right), 86 (top); Brent Winebrenner: 72 (center); **Erich Lessing/Art Resource, NY:** 84; **Musee Dubardo, Tunis/Bridgeman Art Library:** 6 (top); **Photri, Inc.:** 39 (bottom); **SuperStock:** contents (bottom left & bottom center), 5, 11 (center), 21 (bottom), 26 (top), 28, 30 (bottom), 32, 33 (top), 34 (top), 35 (bottom), 37, 39 (top), 43 (bottom), 51, 52 (bottom), 54 (top), 55 (top), 63 (top right), 69 (bottom), 77, 78, 86 (bottom), 88, 97 (bottom), 98 (top), 105, 106, 109, 111, 113 (bottom), 115 (bottom), 117, 122 (top & bottom right), British Library, London: 6 (bottom); Rosenth: 122 (bottom left); **Tony Stone Images:** Gay Bumgarner: 42; Willard Clay: 26 (bottom); Sue Cunningham: 90 (top); Wayne Eastep: 97 (top); Chad Ehlers: 101 (top); Robert Frerck: 90 (bottom); Yann Layma: 122 (center); Cathlyn Melloan: 63 (right center); John Running: 48 (bottom); Hugh Sittion: 94; Art Wolfe: contents (top left), 47.

Map and Chart Illustrations: Thomas Cranmer; Karen Minot.

Additional Illustrations: Brad Gaber; Mike Garner; Bob Masheris; Anita Nelson; Lorie Robare.

Contents

About This Book

Homework takes time and a lot of hard work. Many students would say it's their least favorite part of the school day. But it's also one of the most important parts of your school career because it does so much to help you learn. Learning gives you knowledge, and knowledge gives you power.

Homework gives you a chance to review the material you've been studying so you understand it better. It lets you work on your own, which can give you confidence and independence. Doing school work at home also gives your parents a way to find out what you're studying in school.

Everyone has trouble with their homework from time to time, and *Handy Homework Helper: Geography* can help you when you run into a problem. This book was prepared with the help of educational specialists. It offers quick, simple explanations of the basic material that you're studying in school. If you get stuck on an idea or have trouble finding some information, *Handy Homework Helper: Geography* can help clear it up for you. It can also help your parents help you by giving them a fast refresher course in the subject.

This book is clearly organized by the topics you'll be studying in Geography. A quick look at the Table of Contents will tell you which chapter covers the area you're working on. You can probably guess which chapter includes what you need and then flip through the chapter until you find it. For even more help finding what you're looking for, look up key words related to what you're studying in the Index. You might find material faster that way, and you might also find useful information in a place you wouldn't have thought to look.

Remember that different teachers and different schools take different approaches to teaching Geography. For that reason, we recommend that you talk with your teacher about using this homework guide. You might even let your teacher look through the book so he or she can help you use it in a way that best matches what you're studying at school.

Introduction to Geography

What Is Geography?

When you think about the subject of geography, maybe you think about where a place is and who lives there. The field of geography includes these facts, but it also includes much more.

Geography is the study of the features of the earth and the location of living things on the planet. Geographers study rivers, mountains, plants, and other physical features of the earth. They examine where and how people live. They determine how people change to suit their environments and how people change their environments. For example, geographers studying the city of San Diego might examine its climate, its location near the Pacific Ocean, and its other physical features. They might study how these features have affected the people of the city and their ways of life. They might also examine how people have changed the environment of the area.

Geography can be as simple as studying the path of a stream in your neighborhood and the life in that stream. It can be as complex as using a satellite to study earth's pollution.

Finding Out About the Earth

The word "geography" comes from the Greek word *geographia*, which means "earth description." The ancient Greeks were the first people to study geography in an organized way. They tried to explain the relationship between the physical features of a place and the lives of the people there. Other peoples, such as the Egyptians, Phoenicians, and Arabs, were great travelers and traders. As they traveled, they learned more about the earth. The ancient Romans also added to the knowledge of earth's geography. During the Middle Ages, much knowledge of geography was lost. Later, the 1400s and 1500s were a time of

This Roman mosaic depicts an ocean-going Greek vessel. The Greeks were the first to study geography.

A map from the 1500s shows the level of geographic knowledge at the time.

great discoveries by European explorers. These centuries brought a huge increase in geographic knowledge.

From as early as around 600 B.C., thinkers such as Aristotle and Ptolemy thought the earth was a sphere (a ball) in space. They were right! Earth is one of nine planets in our sun's solar system. It revolves around a star we call the sun. Earth is covered with water, rock, and soil. It is close enough to the sun to receive warmth and light. But it is far enough from the sun so that temperatures are not too hot for living things to survive. Earth is home to human beings and many kinds of plants and animals.

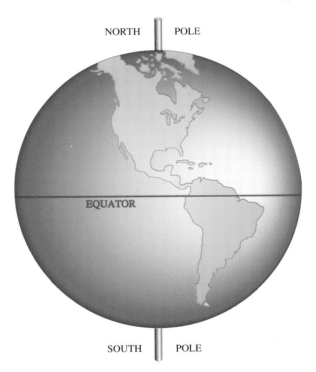

Earth has a **North Pole** at one end and a **South Pole** at the other. The planet is not perfectly round but is slightly flat at the poles. Halfway between the two poles is an imaginary line that circles the earth. This line is called the **equator**.

Location

Our Home, Earth

The earth's surface is composed of about 71 percent water. Almost all the water is in the oceans. An **ocean** is a huge body of salt water. Together, the oceans contain about 97 percent of all the water on the earth.

Some people think of the oceans as one huge body of water. However, we usually divide them into four major bodies of water. The Pacific Ocean is the largest, followed by the Atlantic Ocean, the Indian Ocean, and, finally, the Arctic Ocean.

The oceans include smaller bodies of water, such as seas, gulfs, and bays. A **sea** is any body of salt water that is smaller than an ocean and partly or completely enclosed by land.

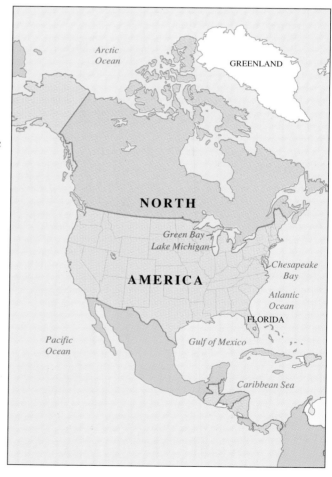

Arctic Ocean

GREENLAND

NORTH

Green Bay
Lake Michigan

Chesapeake Bay

AMERICA

Atlantic Ocean

FLORIDA

Pacific Ocean

Gulf of Mexico

Caribbean Sea

Look on a globe to find the Sea of Japan in the Pacific or the Mediterranean Sea in the Atlantic. Sometimes, however, the word "sea" is used to refer to the oceans in general. A **gulf** is a part of an ocean that extends into land. Examples are the Gulf of Mexico and the Persian Gulf. A **bay** is also a body of water that extends into land. It is smaller than a gulf. A bay may be part of an ocean, such as Chesapeake Bay, or part of a lake, such as Green Bay.

Land makes up 29 percent of the earth's surface. The largest landmasses are **continents.** They are surrounded by water. The largest continent is Asia, followed in size by Africa, North America, South America, Antarctica, Europe, and Australia. Smaller bodies of land completely surrounded by water are **islands.** Islands vary greatly in size. Greenland is the largest island on earth. It covers 840,000 square miles (2,175,600 square kilometers). Some islands are smaller than a city block.

Many continents and islands have **peninsulas,** areas of land that extend out from the rest of the land and are mostly surrounded by water. Most peninsulas, like Florida, are narrow strips of land. The largest peninsula is the Arabian Peninsula, part of Asia. It has about 1,160,000 square miles (3,004,000 square kilometers) of land. Check the map on page 8 to locate examples of different bodies of water and landmasses.

Earth's Size

Circumference around poles: 24,860 miles (40,008 kilometers)

Circumference around the equator: 24,902 miles (40,076 kilometers)

Total area: 196,800,000 square miles (509,700,000 square kilometers)

Water area: about 139,500,000 square miles (361,300,000 square kilometers)

Land area: about 57,300,000 square miles (148,400,000 square kilometers)

Maps: Pictures of Earth

A **globe** lets you see the earth's entire surface. Because it is shaped like a sphere, the globe is the only model that gives a correct picture of the earth as a whole. But a globe cannot fit in a book or give details about a specific place. When you need information from a book or specific information about places on earth, you use a map. A **map** is a flat picture of all or part of the earth.

Globes and Maps

People use maps for many different reasons. You may use a map to help you find your way around a city. Airplane pilots and ship navigators use maps to find their way in air or on water. We can learn about the rivers, lakes, mountains, and even the soil in an area by reading a map. A map can give information about a place's climate, population, industry, and much more.

Lines, colors, and symbols on a map stand for features such as bodies of water, elevations, roads, and cities. You can tell what the lines, colors, and symbols mean by using a map's legend. A **map legend** lists what each symbol stands for. For example, a road map may use one kind of line for highways

Globes	Maps
• duplicate the earth's shape	• show the earth or part of it on a flat surface
• show all land and water surfaces in correct position	• can provide a wide variety of information
• show size and shape in correct proportion	• give detailed information about specific places
• show distance and area without distortion	• can be printed in books

The table lists the strengths of both globes and maps. You can see how globes and maps differ. Maps cannot show true shape, proportion, direction, or distances for all the earth at once. Only globes can show all four of these features correctly at the same time.

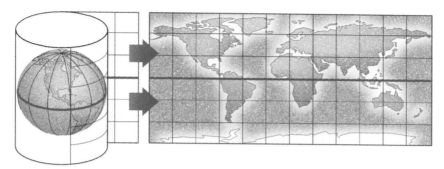

On this map, Alaska looks larger than Mexico. But Mexico is actually larger than Alaska. To show the round earth on a flat map, mapmakers stretch the top and bottom of the map. As a result, places in the far north and south often look larger than places in the middle of the map.

and other kinds of lines to stand for state or county roads. The legend explains what each line means. You need to understand the legend in order to use the map.

Another map feature is called a **compass rose**. It shows the points of the compass. A compass rose shows where to find north, south, east, and west on the map.

A very important map feature is its scale. Maps are just pictures of places on earth. The **map scale** compares the distances shown on maps to the distances in real life. For example, a map may read "1 inch equals about 1,000 miles." This means that one inch on the map

Different types of maps show different types of information. *Top*: A political map shows such data as country borders, capital cities, and major cities. *Bottom*: A terrain map shows mostly mountains, bodies of water, and other land formations.

represents 1,000 miles on earth. A scale may be shown as a ruler that marks off distances along a line.

Words to Know

compass rose: a symbol that indicates direction on a map

map legend: a listing and explanation of symbols and colors on a map

map scale: a line or ratio that shows the relationship of distances on a map to distances on the earth

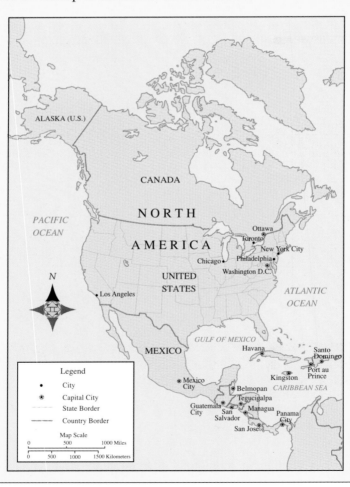

Maps with Grids

Grids are sets of lines that help us locate places on a map. Many maps use an **index grid:** lines that make horizontal rows and vertical columns. The vertical columns are identified by letters that run across the map's top and bottom. The horizontal rows are identified by numbers that run down each side. The map index lists the places on the map and the letters and numbers that identify their location. For example, the index to a map of Mexico might list the city of Guadalajara with the identifying symbol D3. The city is found in the area where the vertical column marked D crosses the horizontal row called 3.

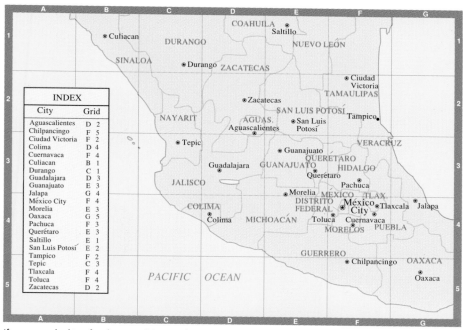

If you were looking for the city of Aguascalientes on this map, you would look at the grid location D2. The city of Oaxaca is at G5.

Latitude and Longitude

By using two grid coordinates, you can locate any point on earth. These two coordinates are latitude and longitude.

Latitude describes the position of any point on earth in relation to the equator. Latitude is measured by parallels. A **parallel** is an east-west line on a globe. Each parallel is the same distance from the parallels on either side of it.

Longitude is measured by meridians. A **meridian** is a line that goes from the North Pole to the South Pole. All meridians meet at the poles.

LINES OF LATITUDE

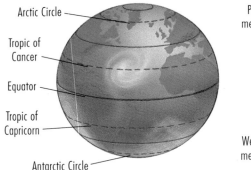

Arctic Circle

Tropic of Cancer

Equator

Tropic of Capricorn

Antarctic Circle

LINES OF LONGITUDE

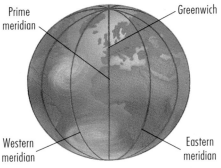

Prime meridian

Greenwich

Western meridian

Eastern meridian

Latitude and longitude are measured in degrees of a circle. Degrees can be divided into smaller units called minutes. The equator has a latitude of 0 degrees. The North Pole has a latitude of 90 degrees north. The South Pole is at 90 degrees south. The latitude of any place between the equator and the poles is between 0 and 90 degrees.

The measurement of longitude begins at the meridian that passes through Greenwich, England. This line is known as the **prime meridian**. It is identified as 0 degrees longitude. The 180-degree meridian lies halfway around the world from the prime meridian. Lines of west longitude lie west of Greenwich. Lines of east longitude lie east of Greenwich.

By identifying the latitude and longitude of a place, we can locate any place on the earth. We use latitude and longitude to find **absolute location**, the exact spot on the earth where a particular place is found. For example, the large city located close to 40 degrees north and 80 degrees west is Pittsburgh, Pennsylvania. You can also identify where Pittsburgh is by giving its **relative location**. The relative location

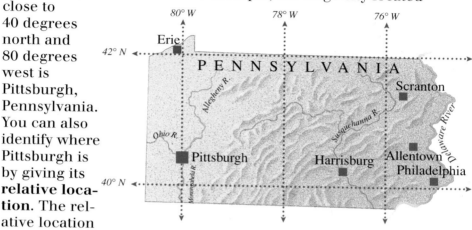

is where something is in relation to other features. For example, you might say that Pittsburgh is in southwestern Pennsylvania where the Allegheny and Monongahela rivers join to form the Ohio River.

Words to Know

absolute location: a place's position on a grid of latitude and longitude lines

latitude: imaginary parallel lines that circle the earth from east to west

longitude: imaginary lines that stretch north and south from the North Pole to the South Pole

meridian: line of longitude running from the North Pole to the South Pole

parallel: line of latitude running east-west around the globe

prime meridian: the 0-degree line of longitude that passes through Greenwich, England

relative location: the position of one place in relation to another place

Hemispheres

The name for any half of the globe is **hemisphere**. The prime meridian divides the Eastern Hemisphere from the Western Hemisphere. It cuts through Europe and Africa. For convenience, geographers say that the Eastern Hemisphere includes all of Europe, Africa, Asia, and Australia. The Western Hemisphere includes North America and South America. Antarctica is in both hemispheres.

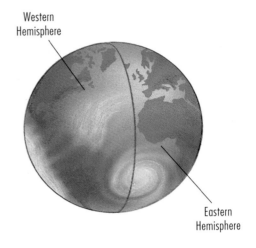

Western Hemisphere

Eastern Hemisphere

The earth can also be divided into the Northern and Southern hemispheres. The equator is the dividing line for these hemispheres. Every place north of the equator is in the Northern Hemisphere, and every place south of the equator is in the Southern Hemisphere.

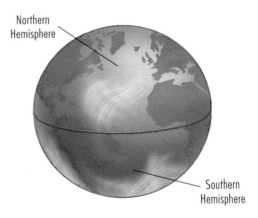

Northern Hemisphere

Southern Hemisphere

If you live in Chicago, Illinois, you live in the Northern and Western hemispheres.

The Physical Environment

Earth's Rotation and Revolution

Earth is one of nine planets that circle the sun. It is the third planet from the sun. A **planet** is a very large body that travels around a star.

Earth is always moving. It spins around on its axis like a top. At the same time, it revolves around the sun.

Imagine a line going through the planet from the North Pole to the South Pole. This imaginary line is called earth's **axis**. The earth spins eastward on its axis, making a complete **rotation** every 23 hours and 56 minutes. The spinning of earth on its axis causes day and night. On the side of earth facing the sun as it rotates, it is daytime. On the side of the earth facing away from the sun, it is night. As the earth turns eastward, people see the sun come up in the eastern sky.

You can demonstrate earth's rotation by shining a flashlight on a globe. Hold the light steady as

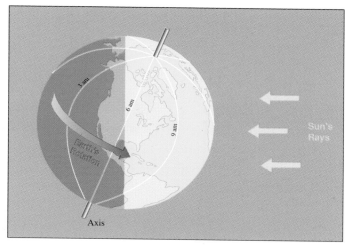

The rotating of the earth on its axis causes day and night. The side of the earth facing the sun is in daytime. It takes 23 hours and 56 minutes to make one complete rotation.

you spin the globe. The area the light is shining on is in daylight. The other side of the globe is in darkness.

While the earth spins, it also slowly **revolves,** or circles, around the sun. If you move a tennis ball (earth) around a basketball (sun), you will get an idea of earth's revolution. The planet completes one revolution in 365 days, 6 hours, and 9 minutes. Earth's path around the sun is called its **orbit.**

The earth revolves around the sun relatively slowly. It takes 365 days, 6 hours, and 9 minutes to make one complete revolution around the sun.

Our 24-hour day and 365-day year are based on earth's rotation and revolution. But one revolution is actually slightly more than 365 days, and one rotation is slightly less than 24 hours. These differences between actual time and calendar time are made up during leap years, which occur every four years.

Words to Know

axis: imaginary line through the earth from the North Pole to the South Pole; earth turns on its axis

orbit: the path of earth around the sun

planet: large body that travels around a star

revolve: to move in a curve around a point; earth revolves around the sun

rotation: the turning of earth on its axis

Seasons

Do you have a favorite season of the year? Perhaps you like the crispness of autumn or the snows of winter best. Or maybe in the place you live, winter is warm and summer is hot. The **seasons** of the year are spring, summer, autumn (or fall), and winter. With each new season,

the weather and amount of daylight change in most parts of the world. The farther you are from the equator, the more seasonal change you will see.

Seasons are caused by earth's tilt on its axis and its movement around the sun. Seasons change because different areas on earth get different amounts of sunlight during the year. Earth is tilted on its axis about 23½ degrees from an upright position. You can demonstrate how different areas of earth receive different amounts of sun by holding a ball at an angle as you circle a lighted lamp. Always face the same direction as you circle the lamp. Do not turn to face the lamp as you move. Notice how one part of the ball gets more light than another at certain times.

During the fall (top) and winter (above) in the Northern Hemisphere, the temperatures are cool and there is less direct sunlight.

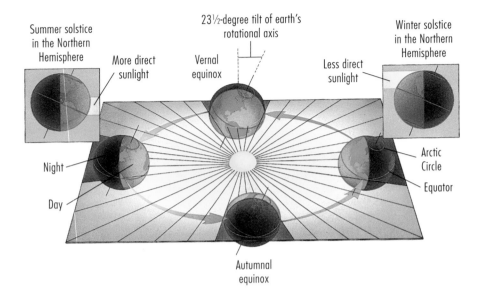

Summer solstice in the Northern Hemisphere

More direct sunlight

23½-degree tilt of earth's rotational axis

Vernal equinox

Less direct sunlight

Winter solstice in the Northern Hemisphere

Night

Day

Arctic Circle

Equator

Autumnal equinox

The Northern Hemisphere tilts away from the sun during the winter. It receives less direct sunlight and has cooler temperatures than at any other time of the year. It tilts toward the sun during the summer. During this time, the Northern Hemisphere receives more direct sunlight and has warmer temperatures.

Geographers and other scientists mark the beginning of each new season by earth's position in relation to the sun. The beginning of spring in the Northern Hemisphere is marked by the **vernal equinox** on March 19, 20, or 21. The **autumnal equinox**, the beginning of autumn, occurs on September 22 or 23. During an equinox, the sun appears directly above the equator. On these days, all places on earth have a 12-hour day and a 12-hour night.

In the Northern Hemisphere, summer begins on the summer solstice, June 20 or 21. On this day, the hemisphere gets more hours of daylight than on any other day of the year. The sun's rays at noon shine directly over the line of latitude at 23 degrees 27 minutes north. This parallel is called the Tropic of Cancer. The winter solstice, December 21 or 22, is the first day of winter in the Northern Hemisphere. On this day, the hemisphere gets the fewest hours of daylight than on any other day. During the winter solstice, the noon sun shines directly over the latitude 23 degrees 27 minutes south. This line is called the Tropic of Capricorn. The area between the two Tropics is called the tropical zone. Most areas in the tropical zone are warm all year long.

Tropic of Cancer

Tropic of Capricorn

Did You Know?

When it is summer in the Northern Hemisphere, it is winter in the Southern Hemisphere. If you have a friend in Australia, he or she may be basking in December's hot summer sun as you shiver in December's cold winter wind.

Summer in Australia, which is in the Southern Hemisphere, begins in December.

Weather

Weather is the condition of the atmosphere at a specific time and place. The **atmosphere** is the air that surrounds earth. The weather where you are may be warm or cold, sunny or cloudy, rainy or dry today. Tomorrow, it could be very different. The weather will almost certainly change from season to season.

The weather depends on four factors: temperature, air pressure, wind, and humidity. **Temperature** is based on the sun's heat energy in the atmosphere. Only a tiny amount of the sun's heat energy ever enters earth's atmosphere. Of this heat energy, 34 percent is reflected back into space by clouds and dust; 19 percent is absorbed by the atmosphere, warming the air; and 47 percent reaches earth's surface, warming the surface. (See the illustration below.) The ground and the oceans absorb the heat energy and then eventually release it back into the atmosphere. The atmosphere prevents much heat from escaping back into space.

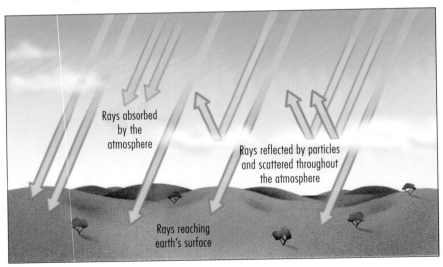

Rays absorbed by the atmosphere

Rays reflected by particles and scattered throughout the atmosphere

Rays reaching earth's surface

The term **air pressure** refers to the atmosphere's force on the earth. Warm air is less dense than cool air. It puts less pressure on the earth. It forms a **low-pressure area**. Cool air puts more pressure on the earth and forms a **high-pressure area**. High-pressure areas tend to push into low-pressure areas.

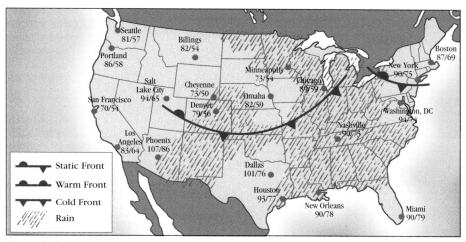

When a high-pressure area (cool air) and a low-pressure area (warm air) move close to each other, a wall called a **front** forms between them. When the cold air mass is advancing, the wall is called a cold front, as shown on this weather map. When the warm air mass is advancing, it is called a warm front.

When air in a high-pressure area moves into a low-pressure area, it creates the air movement you know as **wind**. If two areas have a large difference in air pressure, strong winds will result.

Humidity is the amount of water vapor in the atmosphere. Most water vapor comes from the oceans. If the air contains a lot of water vapor, the humidity is high. Warm air can hold more vapor than cool air. When moist air cools, water vapor may turn into water droplets. The water falls to the earth in the form of rain, snow, sleet, or hail. These types of falling water are called **precipitation**.

Amazing Weather Records

Highest temperature in the United States: 134 degrees Fahrenheit (57 degrees Celsius) in Death Valley, California, July 10, 1913

Lowest temperature in the United States: 80 degrees below zero Fahrenheit (62 degrees below zero Celsius) at Prospect Creek, Alaska, January 23, 1971

Highest wind: 231 miles per hour (372 kilometers per hour) at Mount Washington, New Hampshire, April 12, 1934

Climate

The weather where you live may change from day to day and from season to season. But the climate where you live stays about the same from one year to the next. **Climate** is the average weather conditions in a place over a period of at least 30 years. Many different factors influence the climate of a place.

Latitude is one important factor. It helps determine how warm or cold an area's climate will be. It also influences how much the weather will change from season to season.

Places near the equator, the tropical zones, receive direct overhead heat from the sun throughout the year. These areas have a warm climate. Places near the North and South Poles receive slanted rays from the sun. This indirect light produces less heat than direct rays. The areas close to the poles have colder temperatures. In both polar and tropical areas, the temperatures do not change much in different seasons.

Because of the earth's tilt, places in the middle latitudes have more direct sunlight and longer periods of sunlight in the summer than in the winter. So temperatures vary from season to season. Summer brings warmer temperatures. Winters are colder.

The amount of moisture in the air is another factor in climate. Winds blow moist air from the ocean over nearby land. Over land, it becomes precipitation. Warmer air can hold a lot more water vapor than cool air. So areas near the warm oceans around the equator have the most precipitation. The cold places near the poles have the least precipitation. Also, coastal areas may be cooler in summer and warmer in winter than inland areas. That's because the nearby water changes temperature more slowly than land. It helps keep the air temperature of land that is near water more moderate.

Winds also affect climate. Different places on earth have different wind systems. Winds can carry heat and moisture from one place to another. They can also change directions in different seasons. In some seasons they might bring moist air. In others, they might bring dry air.

Finally, differences in altitude affect climate. Air becomes colder as it rises. It cannot hold as much moisture as warm air. Mountains have cooler temperatures and more precipitation than lower-lying places.

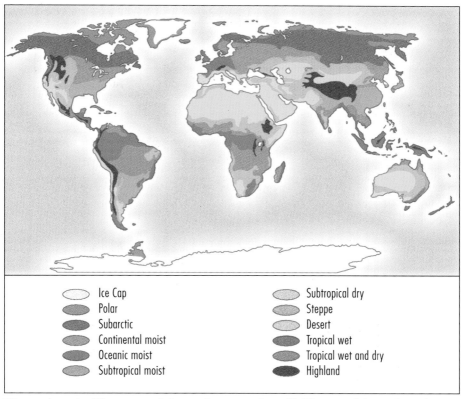

Ice Cap
Polar
Subarctic
Continental moist
Oceanic moist
Subtropical moist

Subtropical dry
Steppe
Desert
Tropical wet
Tropical wet and dry
Highland

This map shows the different types of climates that exist in the world. What type of climate do you live in?

Weathering and Soils

When you plant a seed in a garden or a pot, you put the seed in soil. **Soil** is the material that covers much of earth's land surface. Plants depend on nutrients in the soil for life.

Top: The soil on this soybean farm in Iowa is an example of a **mollisol**, or "soft soil." *Bottom:* The dry soil of the deserts of the southwestern United States is **aridisol**, or "dry soil."

Soil is made up of minerals, decaying plants and animals, water, and air. Earth has many different kinds of soil. Geographers put soils in categories according to color, texture, structure, and chemical makeup. For example, most of the Midwestern prairies in the United States have a soil called a **mollisol**, which means "soft soil." This soil is very rich in plant nutrients. It is excellent for growing crops such as corn or wheat. In fact, prairies are known as the "world's breadbaskets" because of this rich soil. On the other hand, the deserts of the southwestern United States are often known as **aridisols**, which means "dry soil." These soils do not contain as much organic material. It takes a lot of work to grow crops in desert soils.

The rocky, dry soil of this California desert was caused by physical weathering.

What makes soil? Rocks break up through the work of water, ice, plants, or changes in temperature. This process is called **weathering**. Soil results from weathering, acting over long periods of time.

One kind of weathering is **physical weathering**. In physical weathering, rocks break into pieces. Sometimes water fills cracks in rocks and then freezes. As it freezes, the water expands and splits the rocks apart. Roots of trees and other plants may also break rock as they grow in cracks. Physical weathering is common in places where temperatures change greatly over 24 hours. In the dry western United States, days are hot and the nights are cool. Much of the soil there has been formed by physical weathering.

Chemical weathering is caused by water. Water in rivers, oceans, and rainfall dissolves certain minerals from rocks and causes the rocks to break apart. Chemical weathering occurs most often in moist climates. It creates a thick, rich soil. Chemical weathering is common in the eastern part of the United States.

Chemical weathering produced the rich soil on this West Virginia farm.

Erosion and Deposition

The face of the earth is constantly changing. Water and other natural forces break down rock and create soil through weathering. At the same time, water, ice, and wind wear down mountains, create new valleys, and wash away fertile soil. This process is called **erosion**.

Water causes much erosion. The weathering process is one form of erosion. Water also moves rocks and soil from one place to another. As rainwater fills streams and rivers, the moving water flows downhill and cuts into the land.

Have you ever visited the Grand Canyon? This spectacular site is one example of land eroded by water. The Colorado River carved out the canyon over millions of years.

The ocean also causes erosion, changing the land along the seashore. The eroding action of waves and tides creates beaches and cliffs in coastal areas. Glaciers have also carved the landscape through erosion.

The Colorado River began breaking down rock in the Grand Canyon 5 million years ago.

Wind erosion occurs when strong winds blow dust, sand, and soil. The wind changes the landscape by moving these materials from one place to another. In addition, strong winds carry

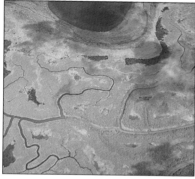

Top left: Wind erosion formed these sand dunes in Death Valley, California. *Above:* A mudslide is another form of erosion, which often results in the destruction of property. *Bottom left:* A **delta** is the area of land built up at the mouth of a river. This is called **deposition**.

particles of sand. When the winds blow, the particles rub against rocks and wear them down.

Landslides and mudslides are dramatic forms of erosion. They change the shape of mountains and valleys.

Sometimes erosion in one place causes a buildup of land in another. For example, a **delta** is a fan-shaped area near the mouth of a river. Mud and other materials are deposited by the river in the delta. Or, the wind may blow sand from one part of a coastal area to another, forming sand dunes. This process of land buildup is called **deposition**.

The Earth's Highs and Lows

Highest land: Mount Everest, 29,028 feet (8,848 meters) above sea level

Lowest land: shore of the Dead Sea, about 1,310 feet (399 meters) below sea level

Deepest part of ocean: Mariana Trench, Pacific Ocean, southwest of Guam, which descends to a depth of 36,198 feet (11,033 meters) below the surface

Landforms

If you visit Death Valley in California, you would be at one of the lowest land areas in the world. If you climbed to the peak of Mount Everest in Nepal, you would be at the highest land area in the world. Mountains and valleys are **landforms**, or natural features of the land's surface. Landforms are the shape of earth's surface, including natural features such as mountains, plains, valleys, and hills.

The word **elevation** describes the distance above or below sea level of a landform. Mount Everest has the highest elevation in the world: 29,028 feet (8,848 meters) above sea level. A place in Death Valley has the

Left: Mount McKinley, Alaska, the highest peak in North America, is 20,320 feet (6,194 meters) above sea level. *Below:* Death Valley was named by pioneers on their way to California because of its barren terrain. It includes the lowest point in the Western Hemisphere.

A **relief map** shows land features such as mountains, plateaus, and valleys.

lowest elevation in the Western Hemisphere: 282 feet (86 meters) below sea level.

Relief refers to the high and low levels of land. Relief is the vertical distance between the highest and lowest points in a specific landscape.

Some maps show land features such as high mountains and low valleys. These are called **relief maps**. Relief maps show elevation as well as relief. Some relief maps use lines and colors to show elevations. Others are three-dimensional, using bumps and grooves to illustrate mountains and valleys. A three-dimensional map is called a **raised relief map**.

The shore of the Dead Sea is the lowest land area in the world.

Mountains, Plateaus, Hills

Have you ever wondered about the difference between a mountain and a hill? In general, a **mountain** is defined as an area that is much higher than its surroundings. Geographers define a mountain as a landform that includes two or more different zones of climate and plant life at different altitudes. In most

Mount Athabasca in Alberta, Canada, towers above its surroundings.

parts of the world, this means that a mountain must be at least around 2,000 feet (600 meters) above its surrounding area. A mountain has steep slopes and peaks that are sharp or slightly round.

The tundra-like area near La Cumbre, Bolivia, is called the Altiplano.

The environment on the highest mountains includes a cold, snowy climate near their peaks where very few plants and animals can live. The next level down is **tundra**, a barren, rocky area. A tundra has some shrubs and mosses. A few animals such as mountain goats and sheep may live here. A timber line divides this area from land on which trees grow. Below this line there may be vibrant forests where plants and animals thrive.

A **hill** is also an elevated landform. It has a distinct summit, or top, but it generally has a relief of less than 1,000 feet (305 meters) Hills and mountains are formed differently and are made of different types of rocks and soil.

This lush green hill with its rich soil is in New Zealand.

Another kind of elevated landform is a plateau. A **plateau** usually has a relief of between 300 feet (91 meters) and 3,000 feet (910 meters). It does not have a sharp peak but covers a wide area. A high plateau is located in North America between the Rockies and the Sierra Nevada ranges.

The Roan Plateau near Douglas Pass in Colorado covers a large area near the Rocky Mountains.

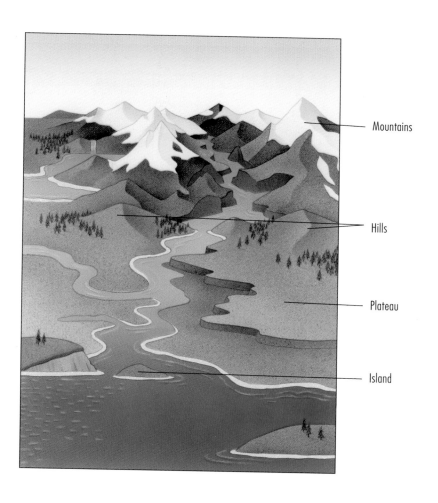

Mountains

Hills

Plateau

Island

Valleys and Plains

A **valley** is a place that has a lower elevation than the ground around it. Valleys are often found between hills or mountains. Many have rivers that drain inland areas to the ocean. Valleys are often formed by the course of rivers and streams and the erosion of the land around them. The flat bottom of a valley is called a **floor**. Valley floors are usually very fertile. People often farm valley floors. A valley floor along the banks of a river is called a **floodplain**. When the river overflows its bed, it floods the surrounding land. The sides of a valley are called **walls** or **slopes**.

An especially deep valley with steep walls is called a **canyon**. The Black Canyon is located in Colorado.

A **canyon**, such as the Grand Canyon in Arizona, is an especially deep valley with steep walls. A valley that is located on a coastline and flooded by the ocean is called a **drowned valley**. Chesapeake Bay is a drowned valley.

A valley may also be located between plains. A **plain** is a wide stretch of land with a level elevation and little relief. A **coastal plain** is a broad, flat stretch of land along an ocean. A coastal plain slopes gradually toward the ocean. Plant life on an inland plain depends on its climate. An inland plain in a humid area may have lush forests. The plains in a dry climate are usually covered with grasslands. The Great Plains in the United States are a dry, grassy plain.

The Great Plains of the United States are home to wheat farms and grasslands.

Above: Dairy cattle are raised in Switzerland, where grass and clover grow in the narrow, steep valleys. *Right:* Cattle are also raised in the Shenandoah Valley, which is located on a flat floodplain.

Switzerland is a country with huge mountains that rise as high as 15,000 feet (4,572 meters) above sea level. Farmers there have a hard time tilling the soil of extremely narrow, steep valleys. Grass and clover grow well, however, so many Swiss farmers are dairy farmers.

Dairy cows are raised in the Shenandoah Valley in Virginia, also. This land is located on the floodplain of the Shenandoah River. It is much flatter than the land in Switzerland. Floods are not always bad news to the farmers here. The water helps spread nutrients throughout the soil. However, every few years the rainfall may be much higher than average. Then, a flood may damage crops, buildings, and animals.

Coasts

You have seen how wind and water erosion change earth's surface. Because a coastline is the area where the land and the water come together, it is a place that is constantly changing.

The land area next to the ocean may be high, rocky cliffs or wide, sandy **beaches**. Beaches may contain black sand from volcanic materials, white sand from the shells of marine animals, or rocks ranging from gravel to boulders.

Winds create waves that change beaches and wear away cliffs. **Tides** also change the coastline steadily day after day. Tides are the rise and fall of the water in the ocean. They are caused by the moon's gravity pulling up the water directly beneath it. When the moon's gravity pulls the water up, a high tide results. At the same time, a high tide occurs on the opposite side of the planet because the moon pulls the earth away from the water there. The action of tides causes the water in the oceans to rise gradually for six hours, until it reaches high tide. The water then slowly goes back down. It reaches its lowest point, low tide, in another six hours. Then the cycle begins all over again. Most coastal areas have two high tides and two low tides each day.

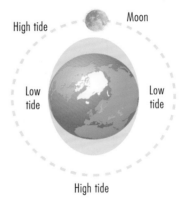

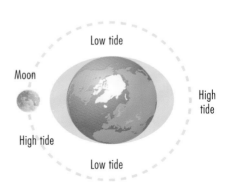

The pull of the moon's gravitational force (gravity) causes high and low tides in earth's oceans and seas.

One interesting kind of coastal area is the **tidal marsh**. A tidal marsh is found inland from a beach. The place must be low and flooded by high tides some of the time. The first area of a tidal marsh is the tide flats. Tide flats are next to the sea floor and are exposed only at very low tides. The low marsh areas farther inland are exposed during low tide and flooded during high tide. The high marsh areas are flooded only at very high tides. These areas have been considered to be wasted land in the past. They have been developed for use as garbage dumps, airports, and even sports stadiums. However, tidal marshes

Tidal marshes (top) and coral reefs (bottom) are two kinds of coastal areas.

have a unique ability to hold water. They help refill ground water supplies. They also have a rich nutrient supply that allows many plants and animals to flourish.

Another type of environment that forms between land and water is a coral **reef**. Coral is made up of the hard outer skeletons of small ocean organisms. New organisms live on top of the shells of dead organisms. Over time, they build up a large structure. Reefs form in warm, tropical seas. When a reef breaks the water's surface, a thin soil can form on top. The reef then becomes home to tropical vegetation. A coral reef can shelter a diverse community of tropical fishes and other organisms.

Glaciers and Glaciation

Many of the world's hills, mountains, and valleys were shaped by **glaciation**, the action of glaciers.

Glaciers are made of snow that has partially melted and refrozen. As new snow is added to the old snow, the air is squeezed out, eventually turning the snow to glacial ice. In Alaska, glacial ice forms quickly, over about 30 to 50 years. Alaska receives a great deal of new snow every winter. The snow does not melt completely over the summer, and the layers build up from year to year. In Antarctica, temperatures stay extremely cold but very little snow falls. Also, the snow rarely melts, even partially. Antarctic glacier ice may take 3,500 years to form. Many places in North America receive several feet of snow every winter, but they do not have glacial ice. That is because the snow melts completely every summer.

Once glacial ice is formed into a body, the body of ice may begin to move. At this point the ice is called a glacier. A glacier may move as slowly as 1 to 2 inches (3.5 to 5 centimeters) a day. Sometimes, a glacier will **surge**, suddenly moving faster than 100 feet (30.5 meters) per day.

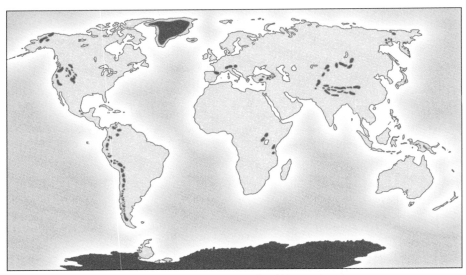

The world's continental glaciers are located in the areas colored blue on this map.

A **valley glacier**, such as Hailugou Glacier in Sichuan Province in China, looks like a river of ice.

The two main kinds of glaciers are valley glaciers and continental glaciers. A **valley glacier** is like a river of ice, following a channel down a mountain. Most valley glaciers are less than 2 miles (3.2 kilometers) long. The Hubbard Glacier in Alaska, however, is over 200 miles (320 kilometers) long. Valley glaciers are also known as **alpine glaciers**.

Continental glaciers are large, thick ice sheets. These are the largest glaciers. They are also called **icecaps**. Continental glaciers bury both valleys and mountains. Greenland and Antarctica have large icecaps. Greenland is covered by one continental glacier. Antarctica is covered by two. The Greenland glacier is more than a mile (1.6 kilometers) deep in some places.

Greenland is covered by one huge **continental glacier**, or **icecap**.

Glaciers change the earth's surface through erosion and deposition. Moving ice picks up rocks that grind the solid rock beneath it. It also pushes rocks and soil ahead of it and gouges out low areas. The moving ice may deposit the rock material in ridges or hills as it melts.

The Water Cycle

On earth, there is more water than any other substance. The oceans are massive bodies of salt water, and glaciers are huge bodies of frozen water. Water fills lakes, ponds, rivers, and streams. Even the air we breathe contains water. Earth's water moves in a continual cycle from the surface to the air and back to earth. This circular movement of water is called the **water cycle** or the **hydrologic cycle**.

1. The heat from the sun warms the earth's surface and air above it.

2. This heat causes water to **evaporate**, or form invisible water vapor. Water evaporates from the oceans, lakes, and rivers. Water also evaporates from the land and living things, such as plants.

3. The water vapor cools and **condenses**, or forms small droplets of liquid water on dust and dirt in the atmosphere. These droplets come together as clouds.

4. As the clouds become cooler, the water droplets become heavier. They fall to the ground as rain, snow, sleet, or hail. Rain, snow, sleet, and hail are called **precipitation**.

5. Most precipitation falls into the oceans. Some falls into lakes and rivers that flow into the oceans. Precipitation that falls on the land may **run off** into rivers and streams. Or it may soak into the ground where plant roots can absorb it. Some of the water that soaks into the ground becomes part of the **groundwater**. Groundwater takes up the spaces between underground gravel or rock layers. The groundwater moves very slowly into lakes and rivers and eventually drains into the oceans.

Step 1. Heat from the sun warms the earth's surface and air above it.

Step 3. Warm, moist air rises and cools as it moves upward. Water vapor condenses into clouds.

Step 4. Precipitation forms and falls.

Step 2B. Water from living things transpires (is released as water vapor) into the air.

Step 2A. Water from oceans, lakes, rivers, and the ground evaporates (becomes water vapor) into the air.

Step 5. Runoff precipitation flows into rivers, lakes, and underground reservoirs (aquifers) and back to oceans.

Freshwater Ecosystems

Freshwater is water that is not salty. Much of the earth's freshwater is in lakes, ponds, streams, and rivers. A **lake** is a body of water that is surrounded by land. A **pond** is a small lake that has shallow water. A **river** is a body of water that flows over land in a long channel. **Streams** are small, often fast-moving, channels of water that combine to form a river.

Teeming with life, ponds feature a variety of plants and animals, such as frogs.

Most of earth's freshwater is in the form of icecaps, glaciers, and groundwater. Only a very small percentage is found in ponds, lakes, rivers, and streams. See the chart on the opposite page to compare the amount of earth's freshwater to saltwater, and to understand where that freshwater is located. Like the oceans, bodies of freshwater are filled with life.

Lake Facts

Largest lake in the world: Caspian Sea, 143,250 square miles (371,000 square kilometers)
Largest Great Lake: Lake Superior, 31,700 square miles (82,100 square kilometers)
Largest lake entirely in the United States: Lake Michigan, 22,300 square miles (57,760 square kilometers)
Deepest lake: Lake Baikal in Russia, 5,315 feet (1,612 meters)

River Facts

Longest river on earth: Nile, 4,145 miles (6,671 kilometers)

Longest river in the United States: Missouri, 2,540 miles (4,090 kilometers)

Second longest river in the United States: Mississippi, 2,340 miles (3,766 kilometers)

River carrying the most water: Amazon in South America

Ponds, in particular, have a vast variety of plants and animals. The shallow waters of ponds allow sunlight to reach the bed, or bottom, of the pond. Plants with roots can grow there. As a result, ponds attract many animals that feed on the plants, and these animals, in turn, attract animals that feed on them. In or near a pond, you might find frogs, toads, mosquitoes, ducks, minnows, and many other species.

Rivers are also home to an amazing variety of life. In the Mississippi River, the huge paddlefish can grow to up six feet in length and weigh 200 pounds. Other types of fish located in various rivers include trout and salmon. The fish eat insects or other fish. In turn, they might be eaten by bears or other predators, or even caught by human anglers.

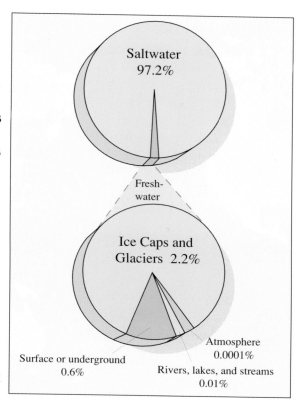

Saltwater 97.2%

Freshwater

Ice Caps and Glaciers 2.2%

Atmosphere 0.0001%

Surface or underground 0.6%

Rivers, lakes, and streams 0.01%

Coho salmon swim upstream in an Alaskan river.

Words to Know

lake: body of water surrounded by land

pond: small lake with shallow water

river: body of water that flows over land in a long channel

stream: small, fast-moving channel of water

World Biomes

A **biome** is a plant and animal community that thrives in a large geographical area. Many geographers identify six major biomes. These are tropical forest, desert, grassland, temperate forest, boreal forest or taiga, and tundra.

A biome has specific kinds of plant and animal life. It is also defined by its climate. For example, the temperate forest biome is found in the eastern half of the United States. This biome is moist, with cold winters and warm summers. Trees such as elm, maple, and oak grow well in this environment's soil and climate. Deer, raccoons, squirrels, and other animals are native to the area. Europe has a climate similar to the eastern United States. It also has a large temperate forest biome.

The way plants and animals relate to one another is an important element of the biome. Each plant and animal occupies a **niche**. A niche is an organism's role in its environment. It includes where the organism lives and what it feeds on. For example, cattle graze on grasses in the grasslands biome of North America. Kangaroos graze in the grasslands of Australia. The two animals are **ecological equivalents**: they occupy the same niche in different places.

Tropical Forests

If you have seen movies that take place in a tropical rain forest, you may picture this biome as a sweltering jungle overgrown with lush vegetation. The facts about tropical forests may surprise you.

The tropical forest climate has the least change in moisture and temperature from season to season. The

Most of the Amazon tropical rain forest is located in Brazil, but large portions also exist in neighboring Peru, Colombia, and Ecuador.

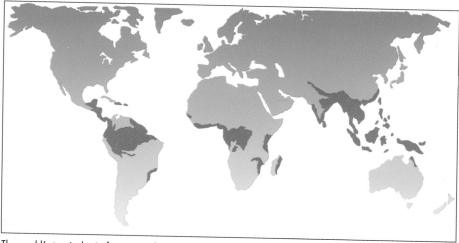

The world's tropical rain forests are located in the areas colored red.

tropical forest biome is found between the Tropic of Cancer and the Tropic of Capricorn. Because the sun's light is evenly distributed all year in the areas around the equator, the forests stay quite warm. But they almost never get as hot as places such as Dallas, Texas, or Atlanta, Georgia, in summer.

Many tropical forests are rain forests. The average temperature in a rain forest is at least 75° Fahrenheit (24° Celsius). A rain forest receives from 80 to 288 inches (203 to 732 centimeters) of rain per year. Five out of every seven days rain falls for part of the day.

Tropical rain forest biomes have different layers of plant growth. The top layer, the **emergent layer**, consists of trees that rise above the rest of the forest. In the rain forest, these trees range from 130 to 250 feet (40 to 76 meters) in height.

The next level down is the **canopy**. The tops of the trees in the canopy are very close. They form a kind of green roof over the forest. The canopy absorbs much of the sunlight received by the forest. It cools the forest floor during the day and keeps warmth in at night. Because of the light-absorbing canopy, little vegetation grows on the ground. That's why the lush jungles you may have seen on television do not exist on the rain forest floor. They are only found near rivers or in areas that have been cleared.

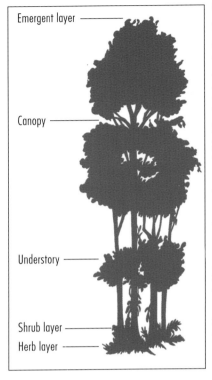

Emergent layer

Canopy

Understory

Shrub layer

Herb layer

The next layer down is called the **understory**. It is made up of the tops of young trees, the trunks of tall trees, and smaller trees. The next layer, the **shrub layer**, is about 20 to 30 feet (6 to 9 meters) off the ground and includes the few shrubs that can find enough light filtering down through the canopy. On the ground is the **herb layer**, made up of small plants that could not survive the elements without the canopy's protection.

Because it is never cold or dry in the tropical rain forest, a huge variety of plant species grow there. Many different animals feed on the plants. In fact, more than half the world's plant and animal species live in the rain forest.

Other tropical forests that are not rain forests exist in places such as southern Asia. These areas are dry for three or four months of the year and then experience extremely heavy rains for several months. Because of these heavy rains, the forest vegetation is similar to that of tropical rain forests. Other tropical forests exist on the middle slopes of some mountains in tropical areas. These forests have trees like those in rain forests. But winds and cooler temperatures prevent the great diversity of plant and animal life found in the rain forest.

The Amazon Tropical Rain Forest

The largest tropical rain forest, the Amazon, covers about a third of South America. In one square mile (2.6 square kilometers) of Amazon forest, scientists have found over 3,000 species of plants. This area is home to exotic plants such as water lilies over 6 feet (1.8 meters) across. Animals have adapted to the rain forest environment. The emerald tree boa

The Parson's chameleon can change its skin color.

is a snake that lives in tree branches. Because of its bright green color, it can hide among the leaves and then surprise its prey and squeeze it to death. The sloth hangs upside down from branches with the help of large hooked claws. Chameleons, such as the Parson's chameleon, can lighten or darken their skin to blend into their surroundings. Other rain forest inhabitants include the poison-arrow frog, the toucan bird, and the golden lion tamarin. A huge array of insects also live in the Amazon rain forest. The morpho butterfly is bright blue and has a wingspan of 8 inches (20 centimeters).

You may have heard a lot lately about working to save the rain forest. This is because people are destroying it at an alarming rate. They want to farm or to produce wood for paper and other products. Many people in the Amazon rain forest make a living by cutting down trees. The trees are used to produce paper, mostly for people in countries such as the United States and Japan. People of many nations are working together to find ways to live off the rain forest without destroying it. These include getting rubber from trees, gathering nuts and fruits, and raising fish and turtles in rain forest streams.

The poison in the tiny poison-arrow frog is one of the world's strongest natural poisons. The frog is brightly colored to warn predators that its skin is deadly poisonous.

Deserts

Deserts seem like harsh, difficult places to live. But some plants and animals have adapted to the hot, dry conditions of the desert biome. A desert is an area that receives an average

of less than 10 inches (25 centimeters) of rain per year. The rains in a desert are usually not evenly spaced throughout the year. Instead, long dry spells are followed by pouring rain. Many deserts are very hot. It is not unusual for the temperature to reach 110° Fahrenheit (43° Celsius), and it may go as high as 125° Fahrenheit (52° Celsius). The desert floor may get as hot

The Sonoran Desert in southwestern United States is famous for its tall saguaro cactuses.

as 175° Fahrenheit (79° Celsius) because it is not shaded by much vegetation. Nights in the desert are cold. The temperature falls as much as 80° Fahrenheit (26° Celsius) at night. This happens because there is little moisture or clouds to hold in the daytime warmth.

You may be familiar with the desert in the western United States. The North American desert is one of the smaller deserts in the world. The largest is the Sahara, in Africa. The Sahara has an area of over 3½ million square miles (9 million square kilometers). About half the continent of Australia is covered by desert.

The desert landscape has many unusual features. Sand covers about 10 to 20 percent of most deserts. The wind blows the sand into large hills called **dunes**. Dunes are constantly changing shape and loca-

The Gila monster of the American Southwest has adapted to the harsh desert climate.

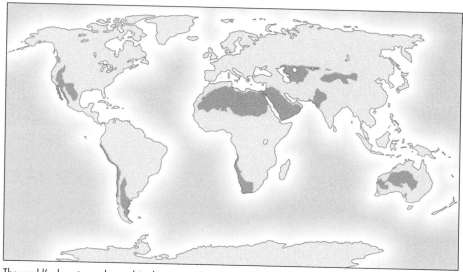

The world's deserts are located in the areas colored orange.

tion. Because the desert is so dry and supports little vegetation, its landscape is easily eroded. One formation, an **arroyo**, is a channel with vertical walls and flat floors. It is caused by flooding that has worn away the soil and rocks. Wind erosion causes desert rocks to take many strange, sculptured shapes. **Mesas** are large, flat hills with steep slopes. They are formed when soft materials wear away and leave behind hard rock. In the middle of the desert's dryness, there are some streams and underground springs. The land around these often forms an **oasis**. This is a green, fertile area.

Desert plants have unusual ways of living in their dry environment. The mesquite tree grows roots 40 feet (12 meters) beneath the ground. These roots draw on water that is hidden far below the surface. Other plants, such as cactuses, store water in their roots, leaves, or stems. Animals, too, must adapt to the desert's harsh environment. One of the best-known desert animals, the camel, may drink as much as 30 gallons (113 liters) of water at one time and then go without water for a week. Other animals survive by avoiding the hot desert floor. They burrow underground during the day or fly high above the heat. Many desert animals only come out at night, when temperatures are cooler.

Grasslands

Natural grassland is any area where only nonwoody plants grow naturally and in plenty. Woody plants are bushes and trees. Nonwoody plants include many kinds of grasses and flowering plants. Most grasslands are in temperate climates that receive between 10 and 30 inches (25 to 75 centimeters) of rainfall per year. That's more rain than deserts and less than forests.

Many areas that are grasslands today are not natural grasslands. They have been formed as people cleared wooded areas to provide land for crops and grazing. Grains such as wheat, rice, and corn are actually types of grasses. That's why grasslands are also important grain-growing regions.

Several different kinds of grasslands are located in different parts of the world. Some are called **prairies** and others are called **steppes**. The prairies of North America are located on continental plains. These are lowland regions with fairly small amounts of rainfall and a long dry season. Some of the American grasslands are described as desert grasslands. They are so dry that only a few species of grass manage to survive.

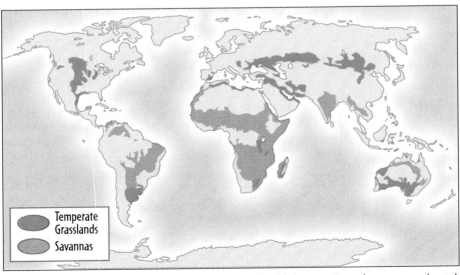

Temperate Grasslands

Savannas

The world's temperate grasslands are located in the areas colored light green. Tropical savannas are located in those colored red.

Top: The Masai steppe in Kenya, Africa, is an example of a grassland. *Right:* Lions roam the African savanna, another type of grassland.

The steppes of Russia are not quite as dry as the desert grasslands. They cover the largest continental plains in the world, stretching 2,500 miles (4,023 kilometers) from the Ukraine to the heart of Asia. These naturally formed grasslands have been developed as farmland only in the twentieth century. They are the natural home of a species of grass that can grow as tall as a human and of bright flowers including wild tulips, anemone, irises, and peonies. These grasslands, like the desert, can be a hostile environment. The summer sun scorches the treeless plains, and the winter winds force small animals into burrows.

The dry-grass plains in the tropics are often classed as **savanna**. The African savanna is located south of the Sahara. It changes from desert-grass savanna to tropical savanna with trees and lush grasses. The acacia is a tree commonly found in the African savanna. Several species of this tall, flat-topped tree grow throughout Africa. In the dry savanna areas, the acacias have developed leaves and roots that help them survive drought. They can also survive fires. Because the savanna has more moisture than other grasslands, it supports a wide variety of plant and animal life.

Fire is important to the grassland biome. Fire prevents dead grasses from building up and releases nutrients from the dead grasses back into the soil. It also helps keep out species from other areas that invade grasslands. Native grasses and plants have adapted so that they can survive fires.

Temperate Forests

The temperate forest biome contains both coniferous and deciduous trees. **Conifers** are evergreen trees, such as pines, firs, spruces, and cedars. Conifers are constantly losing and replacing their leaves, so they appear to be constantly green. **Deciduous** trees, such as oaks, maples, and beeches, lose their leaves every autumn. This helps them avoid losing moisture during the winter months when they cannot get water from the frozen ground. Because deciduous trees have large leaves, they are able to produce more food in the spring and summer.

Temperate forests, such as Glacier Bay Forest, feature coniferous trees or a mixture of coniferous and deciduous trees.

Temperate forests are located mainly in the Northern Hemisphere, in areas with wide seasonal changes. The forests farthest north contain coniferous trees or a mixture of coniferous and deciduous trees. Farther south, many natural forests contain mostly deciduous trees.

A temperate forest goes through dramatic changes with each season. In the autumn, the trees prepare to shut down growth for the winter. The leaves' colors change to bright orange, yellow, and red before they fall.

A gray wolf speaks its mind.

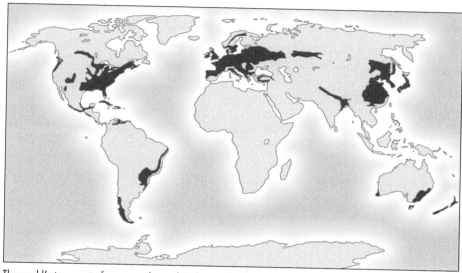

The world's temperate forests are located in the areas colored green.

In the winter, the trees enter a state similar to the hibernation of forest animals. Insects of the forest also die during the winter. But spring brings new insect birth as well as the rebirth of the trees and other plants. In summer, the forest is lush and green.

Temperate forests are home to large animals such as bears, deer, and wolves. Smaller animals such as squirrels, rabbits, raccoons, and opossums also live there. Some of these animals hibernate during the winter. Many birds live in the forests in spring and summer and go south for the winter.

People have a huge effect on the growth of temperate forests. For example, before the Civil War, many of the natural deciduous forests in the South had been cleared for farms. After the Civil War, many plantations were no longer used. The land was planted with pine trees. Now most of the southern forests are coniferous. Today, humans are still a threat to forests. Some forests are cleared for farms, factories, and cities. Pollution from industry endangers forest life. And in some forests, trees are carelessly cut for lumber.

Boreal Forests

North of the temperate forests is a belt of coniferous forests that spreads across the northern continents. This is the boreal forest biome, also called **taiga**. Mountain environments have a timberline, which marks the place above which no trees grow. In the same way, the northern continents have a tree line. No forests are found north of this line. Between the tree line and the temperate forests are the coniferous forests of the taiga.

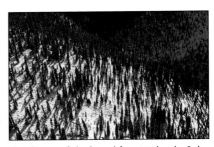
The climate of the boreal forest is harsh. Only a few types of trees are able to survive.

The trees of the boreal forests live in an environment that offers many challenges. The climate brings bitter cold, winds, drought, and snow. The ground has poor, thin soil. The winter lasts eight or nine months, and the growing season is only three to four months long. Because of these harsh conditions, few species of coniferous trees can survive. Many kinds of small mammals live in the boreal forest. These include beavers, porcupines, and rabbits. Ducks, owls, woodpeckers, and other birds also make their home there. Many of these birds travel south for the winter. Large animals in this biome include bears, caribou, and moose.

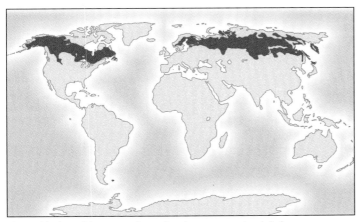
The world's boreal forests are located in those areas colored dark green.

People who live in boreal forests often work in the logging industry. But, the harsh climate and poor transportation in the northernmost boreal forests make logging difficult.

Tundra

North of the tree line in the Northern Hemisphere lies the **tundra**, a barren region. From September through April or May, snow covers the ground. In the summer, temperatures range from 37° to 54° Fahrenheit (3° to 12° Celsius). Even in the summer, the ground from 1 to 5 feet (30 to 150 centimeters) beneath the surface stays frozen. This frozen ground is called **permafrost**. True tundras cover regions in Greenland, Canada, Alaska, Europe, and Asia.

Tundra-like areas are found above the timberline on temperate mountains such as the Rockies and the Himalayas. Although no trees grow in tundra, there is a wide variety of plant life in the summer: mosses, lichens, grasses, flowers, and shrubs. Arctic foxes, bears, and reindeer live in tundra.

A polar bear surveys the tundra.

On the tundra of far northern Canada, the Inuit people have made their home for thousands of years. The Inuits first made their living in this harsh environment by hunting, fishing, and gathering. Now, many of them work in modern industries that mine the tundra's rich mineral deposits.

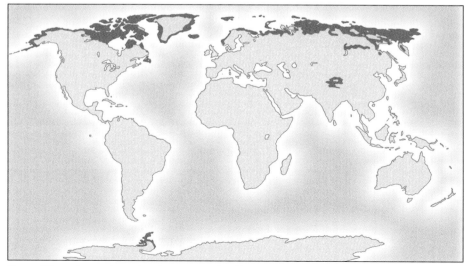

The world's tundras are located in those areas colored blue.

Human Geography

Where People Live and Why

The world population in 1996 was about 5¾ billion people. Studying the world's physical features gives you an idea of the size of our planet and its wide variety of physical features and climates. How do these features affect the places people live?

The world's people are not spread out evenly across the planet. If they were, about 100 people would live on every square mile (2.6 square kilometers) on earth. **Population density** means the average number of people per square mile (or square kilometer) living in an area. People must live in a place where they can produce food or earn money to buy food and other necessities.

Valleys and plains are well populated because they often have fertile land that can be easily farmed. Mountains have fewer people because the soil is thin and easily eroded. Most cities develop near large bodies of water, where major water transportation routes have been established. Cities offer many jobs in trade, industry, business, and transportation. They are more densely populated.

Fertile land and fresh water are **natural resources**. Other natural resources include iron ore, oil, and natural gas. Regions with plentiful natural resources can support large populations. In the past, people could not live very far from natural resources. Now, transportation and communication are much better. Food and fresh water can be carried great distances. Today, populations are still more dense near natural resources, but people can live in places that could not have supported them in the past. For example, many parts of the state of Arizona are dry desert. In the past, these areas could not support a large human population. But today, large cities such as Tucson and Phoenix thrive in the desert.

Climate also plays an important role in population density. For example, no people live in Antarctica year round. Many deserts have few or no people. Europe and southern and eastern Asia have the most densely populated regions in the world. They have temperate or subtropical climates.

The continents of Africa, Australia, and South America have coastal areas with dense populations. The interior areas have sparser populations. North America has densely populated coastal areas and also densely populated central regions.

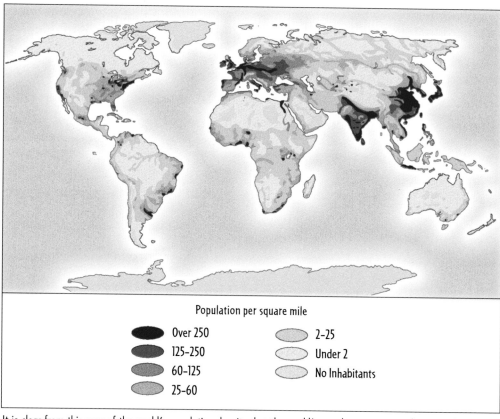

Population per square mile

- Over 250
- 125–250
- 60–125
- 25–60
- 2–25
- Under 2
- No Inhabitants

It is clear from this map of the world's population density that the world's people are not spread out evenly across the planet.

Patterns of Settlement

Have you ever thought about whether you prefer the country, city, or suburbs? Geographers think about this issue also. When they talk about **patterns of settlement**, they mean where people live and how these settlements are distributed. A pattern of settlement may be described as mainly urban, suburban, or rural. The United States has an urban pattern of settlement that is becoming more and more suburban.

An **urban** area, or a **city**, is a densely populated settlement. Cities usually have more than 1,000 people per square mile (2.6 square kilometers). City residents make a living in ways

other than producing food. Since World War I, more and more people in America have moved from rural areas to cities. A city is the center of economic, religious, and social life. A **town** is a similar center that is smaller than a city.

Suburbs are the towns surrounding a large city. There have been suburbs since ancient times when cities had smaller settlements outside their walls. Because they did not have the protection of the walled city, these suburbs were often home to people of less wealth and lower social class. During the Renaissance, wealthy citizens began the trend of building summer homes outside the city.

With a population of 7,322,564 (1990 census), New York City is one of the most densely populated places in the world. It is also an American economic and cultural center.

They wanted to enjoy fresh air and beautiful scenery. During the Industrial Revolution, cities became even more crowded. (See pages 72–73 for more information on the Industrial Revolution.) Transportation also improved. Now people could

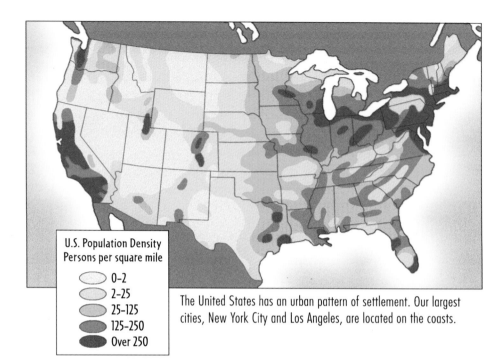

U.S. Population Density
Persons per square mile

- 0–2
- 2–25
- 25–125
- 125–250
- Over 250

The United States has an urban pattern of settlement. Our largest cities, New York City and Los Angeles, are located on the coasts.

live outside the city and travel to and from work on streetcars or railroads. The growth of suburbs in many developed countries continues today.

Rural areas have a less dense population than cities and suburbs. They have large open spaces of land that are often used for farming.

If you live in or near a city, you have probably heard the term **metropolitan area**. A metropolitan area is a city and the suburbs that surround it. The city and suburbs in a metropolitan area are closely connected. People from the suburbs might work in the city. People from both the city and suburbs might shop in the suburbs. "Metropolitan area" is a useful term to describe the community of people who live in and around a city. Some cities have very large metropolitan areas.

Migration

Have you ever been to a Chinatown or a Little Italy? Many American cities have neighborhoods like these, named for the people who live there. **Migration** is the movement of people from one place to a permanent settlement in another place. Migration may be internal, such as when people move from a rural area to an urban one in the same country. External migration is when people move from one country to another one.

When people move away from their country, they **emigrate**. When they move into a new country, they **immigrate**. People leave their home countries for many different reasons. They may leave because it is hard to get food or housing in their home country. Or maybe they cannot find work. They may leave because they are persecuted for their religious or political beliefs. For example, in the 1600s the Pilgrims left England because they were not allowed to worship as they wanted. They settled in Massachusetts, where they could worship and govern themselves as they chose. Today, people in all parts of the world migrate for many of the same reasons as they did in the past.

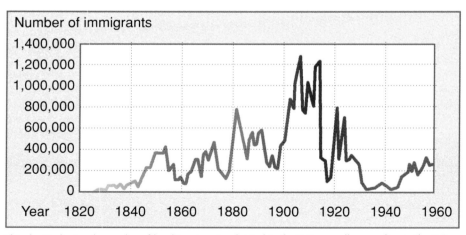

This chart indicates the number of legal immigrants admitted to the U.S. annually, according to the U.S. Immigration and Naturalization Service.

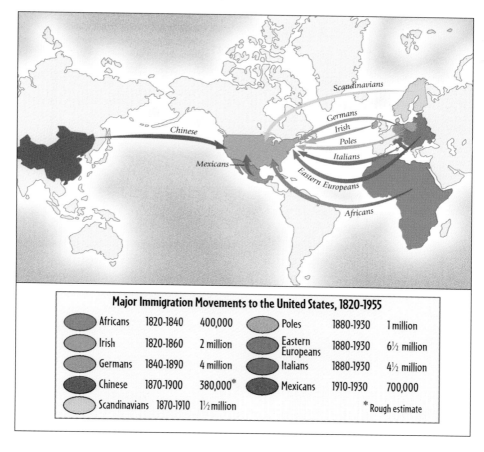

Major Immigration Movements to the United States, 1820-1955

Africans	1820-1840	400,000		Poles	1880-1930	1 million
Irish	1820-1860	2 million		Eastern Europeans	1880-1930	6½ million
Germans	1840-1890	4 million		Italians	1880-1930	4½ million
Chinese	1870-1900	380,000*		Mexicans	1910-1930	700,000
Scandinavians	1870-1910	1½ million				* Rough estimate

Between 1820 and 1955, the United States received more immigrants than any other country. Around 40 million people, mostly from Europe, settled in the United States. In the mid–1800s, over 2 million people immigrated from Ireland alone. In Ireland, many people depended on potatoes for food. When the potato crop failed, 750,000 died of starvation or disease. Many others emigrated. Because many who migrated to the United States had little money, they settled near where they landed, on the East Coast. Because of the famine and emigration, the population of Ireland today is only about half of what it was in 1845.

Natural Increase

Every ten years, the United States government collects information about the country's population. This collection is called a **census**. A census also gathers other important information, such as how old people are and where they live. The study of population and information about people in a population is called **demography**.

The population of a place can become larger or smaller. Birth rate, death rate, and migration cause a population to increase or decrease. **Birth rate** is the number of births per year per 1,000 people. **Death rate** is the number of deaths per year per 1,000 people. To find out how fast a population is growing, demographers subtract a place's death rate from its birth rate. The number they get is called the rate of **natural increase**. It is expressed as a percentage. For example, in 1995, the birth rate in the United States was 15 per 1,000. Its death rate was 9 per 1,000. So its rate of natural increase was 0.6 percent.

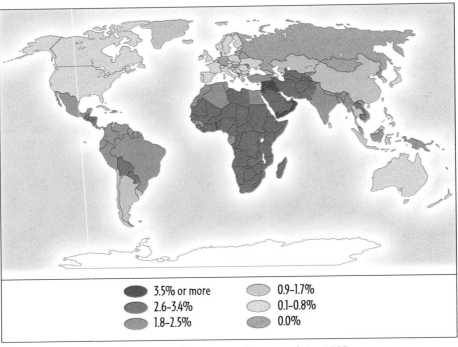

● 3.5% or more	○ 0.9–1.7%
● 2.6–3.4%	○ 0.1–0.8%
● 1.8–2.5%	● 0.0%

This map indicates what the rate of natural increase was by country during 1995.

Demographers look at both natural increase and migration when they calculate how fast a population is growing. To calculate how fast the earth's population is growing, you only need to know the natural increase. No people are emigrating from earth or immigrating to earth!

In 1987, the world's population passed 5 billion people. It is increasing at a rate of about 1½ percent per year. If this rate of population growth continues, the world's population will double every 45 years.

Mexico City (top left), Sao Paolo, Brazil (top right), and old Delhi, India (above), are among the most crowded cities in the world.

Because of improvements in living conditions, the death rate has dropped for the last 200 years. If the rapid population growth continues, some economists think that the world will not be able to feed all the people well. It would not be possible for everyone to have good food or enough shelter. This situation is called **overpopulation**. To fight overpopulation, many governments have urged that people have smaller families. These governments want the birth rate to be the same as the death rate. Some economists do not feel overpopulation will become a problem. They believe that better technology and new inventions will make it possible for the earth to feed its growing population.

World Countries

A **country** is a recognized territory with definite boundaries. Its government legally rules over the people living within the boundaries.

A map that shows the boundaries of counties, states, or countries is called a **political map**. Many different things cause changes in the political map of the world. In the sixteenth through nineteenth centuries, the exploration and settlement

of the New World made many changes in country boundaries. Wars can also make changes in countries and their boundaries. For example, as a result of World War I, many new nations were created in Europe. Austria and Yugoslavia were two of these. In 1991, the Communist government of the Soviet Union fell. This huge country broke into 15 smaller ones, including Russia.

Russia is troubled by many economic problems, which have not been lessened by the fall of Communism. Here peddlers display illegally obtained goods at an open market.

The most common form of government in the countries of the world is democracy. In a democracy, the citizens elect representatives to make and enforce laws. Countries with democratic governments include the United States, Great Britain, Canada, Australia, Japan, and most western European countries. Some countries have **authoritarian** governments. This means that only a few people make government decisions. For example, the Communist Party rules the government of Cuba. Rulers called **dictators** govern some countries in Asia and Africa with the help of their armies.

The Soviet Union broke into 15 separate countries after the Communist government fell in 1991.

Many organizations help countries work together. Nearly every country of the world belongs to the United Nations. The United Nations helps settle disagreements among countries. It helps improve health and education in countries around the world. Other organizations, such as the European Union, help countries do business with each other.

The largest nation in area in the world is Russia. Canada is the second largest. The country with the largest population is China. The two smallest countries are Monaco and Vatican City. Each of these countries has an area of less than 1 square mile (2.6 square kilometers).

States and Provinces

You probably know that some countries are divided into states or provinces. The United States consists of 50 states. A **state** is a unit of regional government within a country. Some other countries that have states are Brazil and India.

The United States has a **federal** system of government. This means that the national government has some powers and the state governments have others. For example, the national government coins money, negotiates with other governments, and controls immigration and emigration. The state governments have authority over public schools, and they make civil and criminal laws. In some situations, the national and state governments both have power. For example, both can collect taxes and build highways.

Some countries, such as Canada and China, are divided into **provinces**. Canada has ten provinces and three **territories**. The territories are areas in far northern Canada with severe

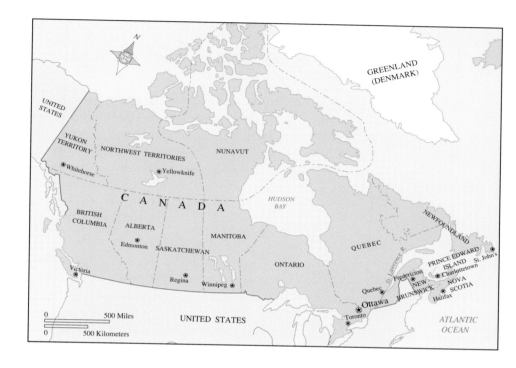

climates and small populations. Canada's provinces are similar to the U.S. states—they have many governmental powers. Those in China, however, have little power.

States and provinces, as well as countries, have a **capital**. A capital is a city where the government has its headquarters. For example, Ottawa, in the province of Ontario, is Canada's capital. The capital of the province of Ontario is Toronto.

Have you ever heard people use the word "state" when they were not talking about one of the 50 United States? The word "state" has more than one meaning. Sometimes, it is used as a synonym for "country." Other times, people use it to mean "government." In a sentence such as, "The state has power over its people," the speaker is talking about a government. This may sound confusing, but it's not. If you pay attention to the rest of the sentence, you will understand what the speaker is talking about when he or she says "state."

Local Political Divisions

States and provinces contain many smaller units of government. These include counties, cities, towns, and villages. If you live in the United States, you might not live in a city, a town, or even a village, but you almost certainly live in a county.

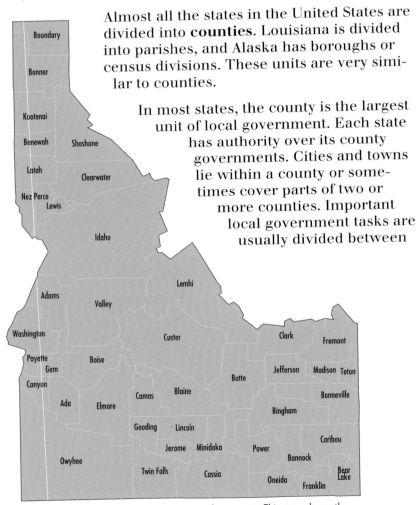

Almost all the states in the United States are divided into **counties**. Louisiana is divided into parishes, and Alaska has boroughs or census divisions. These units are very similar to counties.

In most states, the county is the largest unit of local government. Each state has authority over its county governments. Cities and towns lie within a county or sometimes cover parts of two or more counties. Important local government tasks are usually divided between

A county is a smaller unit of government within a state. This map shows the counties of Idaho.

the county govern-
ment and the city or
town government.
For example, the
county may run the
courts while the city
is in charge of the
fire department and
the police depart-
ment.

Other countries
have different kinds
of local divisions.
For example, Italy
is divided into 20
regions. The regions

Louisiana is divided into parishes instead of counties. The plantation called Oak Alley is located in the St. James Parish.

are divided into provinces, and the provinces are divided into communes.

Alaska is divided into boroughs or census divisions instead of counties.

Economic Activity

You practice economics every day. If you want to buy lunch or a game, you must decide whether you have enough money to pay for it. If you earn some money, you decide how you will spend it. The governments of nations must make these same kinds of decisions.

Long ago, people often got what they needed by direct trade, or bartering. For example, if you had a pig and you wanted a goat, you might make a trade with someone. But this was not always practical. What if the person did not want a pig? The use of money allowed people to buy what they needed. To earn money, you make a product or provide a service. You spend your money on other people's products and services. The study of how goods and services are produced and distributed is called **economics**.

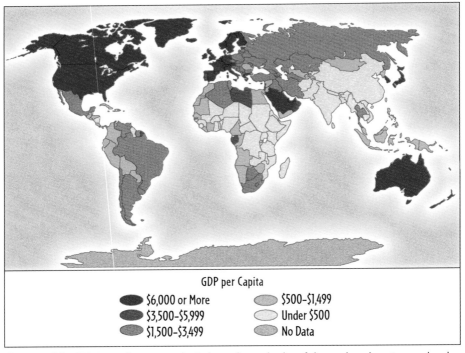

GDP per Capita

$6,000 or More
$3,500–$5,999
$1,500–$3,499
$500–$1,499
Under $500
No Data

This map of the GDP (gross domestic product) shows the total value of the goods and services produced by country in the year 1991.

A country's government has much to do with the country's economy. The government collects taxes, issues money, and provides services. A country's economy can be put into one of three categories based on how much control the government has over the country's businesses. In a **capitalist** economy, private citizens own and run most of the businesses. They decide how much to charge for goods and services. The United States, Canada, and Japan have capitalist economies. In a **socialist** economy, the government owns some of the important industries, such as steel mills and railroads. Private citizens own other businesses. Sweden, Norway, and Israel have socialist economies. In a **communist** economy the government owns and regulates almost all the businesses. China has a communist economy.

The total value of the goods and services produced in a country in one year is called its **gross domestic product**, or **GDP**. This number is stated in dollars. For example, in 1993 the GDP of the United States was $6,343 billion. France's GDP for that year was $1,253 billion. To compare GDP by countries, a number called the **per capita GDP** is used. "Per capita" means "per person." The per capita GDP is the average value of goods and services produced by each person in a country. This number is found by dividing the GDP of a country by its population. The per capita GDP of France in 1993 was $21,930. That means the average French citizen produced $21,930 worth of goods or services.

The countries of the world can be divided into two groups: **developed countries** and **developing countries**. Developed countries have many industries and usually have a higher per capita GDP than developing countries. The United States, Japan, and most of the countries in Europe are developed countries. Developing countries have an economy based more on farming than on industry. They generally have a lower per capita GDP. Most of the world's developing nations are in Asia, Africa, and Latin America. People in developing countries often receive fewer years of education and less advanced health care. It can be hard to get information because there are fewer newspapers, phones, and televisions. Developing countries also usually have higher population growth rates than developed countries.

Economic Diversification

Up until about 10,000 years ago, people spent almost their whole lives searching for food. They wandered over the land, hunting wild animals and gathering wild plants. Then people gradually learned how to grow plants for food. They also began to domesticate wild animals such as sheep, goats, and cattle. That means they tamed the animals and herded them. People settled down to live in one place. As agriculture developed, people produced bigger food supplies. Not everyone had to spend all their time on food production. People were now able to **diversify**: develop other means of making a living. People started to work in crafts and trades. This great change has been called the Agricultural Revolution.

Economic activities are often grouped in four **sectors**. The primary sector is agriculture, mining, forestry, and fishing. The secondary sector is industrial manufacturing. The ter-

tiary (third) sector is services, such as retail stores and banking. The quaternary (fourth) sector is information, including computers and telecommunications.

From the Agricultural Revolution until the 1700s, most people worked in the primary sector. Then came the Industrial

Top: Agriculture, such as rice farming, is part of the primary sector. *Above left:* This woman selling coffee participates in the tertiary sector. *Above right:* The quaternary sector includes computer information services.

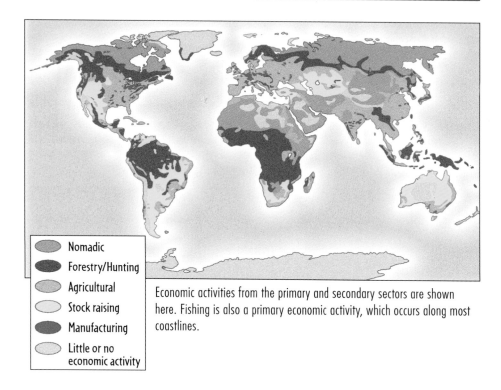

Legend:
- Nomadic
- Forestry/Hunting
- Agricultural
- Stock raising
- Manufacturing
- Little or no economic activity

Economic activities from the primary and secondary sectors are shown here. Fishing is also a primary economic activity, which occurs along most coastlines.

Revolution. In the 1700s, many people went to work in factories instead of on farms. They were working in the secondary sector. To find jobs in factories, people moved from rural areas to cities. As the Industrial Revolution spread, many countries began turning away from an economy based only on agriculture. The United States, Belgium, France, and Germany were among these countries.

Economic diversification continues today. Developing countries have had economies based on agriculture and selling their natural resources, such as lumber. They are turning more to technology and industry, and improving transportation and communications.

Keep in mind that developed countries with jobs in the quaternary sector still have agriculture and manufacturing. Diversification means that a country has industries from all the sectors. This leads to a country that offers a large variety of goods and services. It includes a population that is well educated and can expect to live a longer life.

Agriculture

The development of farming around 10,000 years ago greatly changed people's lives. The industrial age may have given people new ways to earn a living, but farming is still the world's most important industry. More people the world over work in agriculture than in any other industry. About half the workers in the world work in farming.

There are many different kinds of farms in the world. They give us an amazing range of products. If you traveled around the world you might visit a rubber tree farm in Indonesia, a silkworm farm in China, a banana plantation in Brazil, and a sheep ranch in Australia.

The two main kinds of farms are **specialized farms** and **mixed farms**. A specialized farm grows only one **cash crop**: a crop that is grown to sell. Cash crops can be wheat, bananas, rice, sugar cane, or many others. A specialized livestock farm raises cattle, poultry, or sheep. Specialized farms can be risky because disease, insects, or bad weather could wipe out an entire season's production. A mixed farm produces a variety of crops and animals.

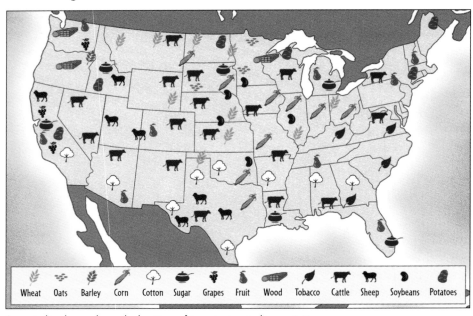

| Wheat | Oats | Barley | Corn | Cotton | Sugar | Grapes | Fruit | Wood | Tobacco | Cattle | Sheep | Soybeans | Potatoes |

An agricultural map shows the locations of important agriculture activities.

More and more, farms in the United States are owned and operated by big businesses. Today there are over 2 million farms in our country. The average size of a farm is about 470 acres. Many farmers sell their produce through contract farming. In **contract farming**, the farmer promises to sell a certain amount of the farm's produce at a specified price. The farmer often sells to companies that sell grain or that make food products.

Farmers decide what to grow based on their environment. They must begin with fairly level land and soil that can be tilled. Some soils are richer in nutrients. Plants grow more easily in these soils. Some soils are better for some crops than for others. Climate is an important factor in deciding which crops to grow. Some crops, such as cocoa beans and sugar cane, grow well in a tropical climate. Others, like potatoes, grow well in a cooler climate. Different crops also need different amounts of sunshine and rain.

Some of the earliest farm inventions were irrigation and the plow (pulled by oxen). **Irrigation** is bringing water to fields that do not get enough water from rain.

Irrigation brings water to fields that do not get enough water from rain.

In the last few centuries, many inventions have helped farmers do their work. The cotton gin, the reaper, the combine, and the steel plow were invented in the 1700s and 1800s. These allowed farmers to produce larger quantities of crops more successfully. The mid–1900s brought electricity to farm equipment. At the same time, scientists improved the breeding of plants and animals. Other scientists developed new fertilizers, insecticides, and herbicides (weed killers).

One of the greatest challenges facing agriculture today is how to increase food production in developing countries. Most developing countries have rapidly increasing populations, and they cannot feed the increasing numbers of people. Many farming improvements have been made, but the problem has not been solved yet. One promising approach is to adapt traditional farming methods to produce more food.

Manufacturing

Manufacturing industries produce goods. Manufactured products may satisfy our basic needs for clothing, food, and shelter. Or they may make our lives easier or healthier. Some manufactured goods are steel, paper, automobiles, shoes, and refrigerators.

Manufacturing industries take raw materials and make a finished product from them. **Raw materials** are things found in nature that are made into manufactured products. Wood is a raw material. The word **output** describes the manufactured products. The word **input** describes the machinery and raw materials used for the product. Five basic inputs are needed for production. The first input is **natural resources**, such as land, water, and minerals. The second requirement for production is **capital**: the thing used to make a product, such as buildings, machines, and trucks. Capital can also refer to the money used to start or expand a business. The third is **labor**, or human input: work done by employees. **Management**, the fourth type, describes the employees who supervise the other employees. Management makes decisions such as how much to produce and what prices to charge. The fifth input is **technology**: knowledge of machines, tools, and how to use them.

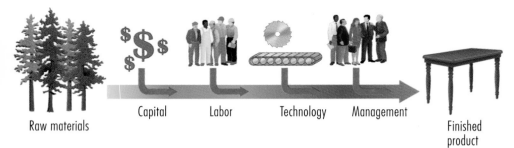

Raw materials   Capital   Labor   Technology   Management   Finished product

Developed countries produce many more manufactured goods than developing ones do. Developing countries often lack the capital, trained labor, and management needed for production. Many of the industries in developing countries

Among those goods manufactured in the United States are cars. This photo of an auto assembly plant shows two of the inputs needed for the production of goods—**labor** and **technology**. Over the years, improvements in technology in some industries have resulted in the replacement of human labor with machines. But, the success of America's manufacturing industries has always been dependent on the skill and hard work of its laborers.

must produce necessities such as food and clothing for their citizens. Many industries in developed countries produce luxuries and products for leisure enjoyment. Manufacturing companies in developed companies often buy raw materials from developing countries to make their products.

Increased manufacturing has made life easier in general. However, there are problems connected to the growth of manufacturing. Factories sometimes pollute the air and water with their waste products. Manufacturing uses up huge amounts of energy. Factories use much petroleum and natural gas, which cannot be replaced.

Services

If you walk down the street in your town or city, you might pass a restaurant, a video arcade, a bank, a doctor's office, or a gas station. These are all **service industries**. Service industries do not make products. They supply services. Some of the categories of service industries are health care, education, automobile services, household services, and recreation.

In the United States, service industries make up about two-thirds of the GDP. (See pages 70–71 for information on GDP.)

In the city of Rhodes, Greece, tourists outnumber the local population by four to one in the summer.

Services have become more important to our economy since the mid-1900s. A country usually develops large agricultural and manufacturing industries then develops its service industries.

Fast-food restaurants are a rapidly growing service industry. Others that continue to grow are computer services, legal services, and health care. Service industries that have decreased in recent years include gas stations and house-cleaning services.

Some countries, such as Greece, base a large part of their economy on the tourist industry. This includes the service industries of hotels and restaurants. Thanks to the booming tourist business, other industries in Greece have also done well. For example, the construction industry is helped by the need to build hotels and restaurants.

Technological Change

Technology means the ways people use inventions and discoveries to make their lives better and easier. Technology increases production and reduces the amount of labor needed. People have always used technology, but technology has changed a lot in the past 50 years. For example, in the United States in the 1800s, animals and people did about 65 percent of the work on farms while machines did 35 percent. Today, machines do 98 percent of farm work. Factory work has changed also. One hundred years ago, people did factory work by hand or with hand-operated machines. They worked up to 96 hours per week. Today, with modern machinery, most factory workers work 40 hours per week.

If you ever play electronic video games, you have seen electronic technology in action. Electronic science is less than 100 years old. Electronic devices are used in televisions, radios, VCRs, computers, robots, X-ray machines, and lasers. The possibilities for these tools seem endless. They help people communicate and get work done. Electronic technology helped create the quaternary economic sector (see page 72). The Internet is a good example of new computer technology that is quickly changing the way people communicate, do business, and get information.

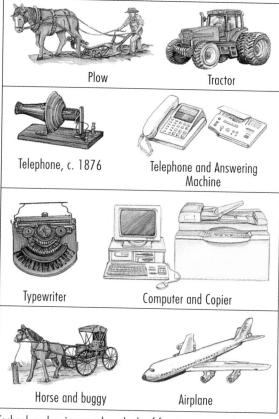

Plow

Tractor

Telephone, c. 1876

Telephone and Answering Machine

Typewriter

Computer and Copier

Horse and buggy

Airplane

Technology has improved methods of farming, communication, printing, and transportation.

Transportation

Transportation is the movement of people and things from one place to another. Transportation takes us to our jobs. It makes it possible for the people of the world to trade with one another. It makes the world seem smaller by taking us to many different places. Modern transportation has brought people closer together in ways people living 200 years ago could only imagine. Trade between countries has become much easier. Because of modern transportation, you can use goods from all parts of the planet.

The first transportation was by foot. People transported themselves and their goods, carrying them on their heads or backs. By about 4000 B.C., people used animals to transport goods. The wheel was invented in Mesopotamia around 3500 B.C. (Mesopotamia is now the country of Iraq.) The wheel transformed transportation. It enabled people to use four-wheeled carts pulled by animals to transport goods. Ancient peoples also used sailing ships. Since they did not have navigation

A Transportation Time Line

Around 3500 B.C.: The first vehicles with wheels are built in Mesopotamia.

About 300 B.C. to 300 A.D.: The Romans build the first large network of paved roads.

1700s: The first steam engine is developed by British inventors.

Around 3200 B.C.: The Egyptians first use sails and make sailboats.

1490s: Better ships and navigation make it possible for ships to travel across the oceans.

instruments, they had to stay within sight of land. In the 1400s, new navigation instruments made it possible for ships to travel farther. Transportation improved in the 1700s and 1800s. People built good roads for horse-driven wagons. Canals also made transporting goods easier.

Many of the greatest leaps in transportation occurred in the last 200 years. The steamboat, the locomotive, the automobile, and the airplane opened the door to modern transportation. Today, automobiles are the most popular form of private transportation. Within and between cities, buses and trains provide **public transportation**: an organized passenger service used by the general public.

Airplanes also provide public transportation. They are also used to transport goods. However, the cheapest way to transport goods is by water. The next cheapest forms are train and truck. Another form of transportation is pipelines. Pipelines carry natural gas and petroleum over long distances.

1903: Orville and Wilbur Wright's airplane makes the first powered flight.

1950s: Passenger airlines begin using jet airplanes regularly.

1890s: The French build the first gasoline-powered automobile.

1920s: Cars become a major means of transportation in the United States.

1981: The first space shuttle is launched.

Communication

Communication is the exchange of information between people through the use of symbols, signs, or behavior. Communication may be spoken or written. One main kind of communication is **interpersonal communication**: face-to-face discussions, telephone conversations, and letters written from one person to another. The second main kind of communication is **mass communication**: messages that are sent out to a large audience through books, magazines, newspapers, radio, and television.

Thousands of years ago people used drumbeats, smoke signals, and fire to send messages in code. With spoken languages, people could speak face-to-face or send runners with verbal messages. Later, horses could speed message-sending.

Picture-writing was invented by the Sumerians in West Asia around 4000 to 3000 B.C. It was a huge advance in communication. It let people preserve messages and communicate without relying on the memory of a messenger. The first writing is called **cuneiform**. It was composed of wedge-shaped characters that stood for syllables.

A Communications Time Line

20,000 B.C.: People painted animals on cave walls.

Around 1040: The Chinese use movable type to make books. This makes it possible to produce books in large numbers.

1600s: Printed newspapers begin to appear in many European cities.

105: Paper is invented in China.

Mid–1400s: Johannes Gutenberg introduces movable type in Europe.

In Europe in the 1400s, mass communication became possible. Books, newspapers, and magazines became increasingly common. However, these could spread through the world only as fast as the day's travel would allow. In the 1700s, news from Washington, D.C., could take up to 44 hours to travel by stagecoach to New York City. When Samuel F. B. Morse invented the telegraph, it was a giant step forward. Messages could arrive in minutes instead of weeks. Alexander Graham Bell's invention transformed communication in the late 1800s. Today the telephone is an important form of interpersonal communication.

Mass communication made great leaps with the invention of radio. The first radio broadcast was made in 1920 in Pittsburgh, Pennsylvania. Radio provided news and entertainment more quickly and more often than the newspapers. When television broadcast the first moon landing in 1969, the wonders of modern mass communication were clear. Television helps people all over the world share the same experiences at the same time.

The computer continues to make communication faster and easier for people everywhere. Information can be shared instantly. This new ability to share information instantly has been called the "Information Revolution."

1936: In Great Britain, the first public television service begins.

1876: Alexander Graham Bell patents the telephone.

1980s: Computers make it possible to transmit messages immediately to any part of the world.

1844: Samuel F. B. Morse sends the first telegraphic message, using the machine he invented.

1901: Guglielmo Marconi, an Italian, transmits a signal in Morse code across the Atlantic Ocean.

1962: The first telecommunications satellite is launched by the United States.

Global Interdependence

"It's a small world." You might use that saying when you meet an old friend in an unexpected place. But with today's advanced transportation and communication, the world seems to be getting smaller and smaller.

The nations of the world have traded with one another throughout history. In the 1400s and 1500s, Europeans traveled to the East to buy silks and spices. Traders made long trips over land or by sea. Today's fast transportation and communications methods make it possible for countries to trade many more goods than ever before.

No one country can produce all the goods people need at reasonable prices. Each country has the resources to produce some goods better than other countries can. For example, the United States grows and produces large amounts of cotton. The cotton is sold to many other countries. However, the United States does not produce enough coffee beans for its citizens. So we buy large amounts of coffee from Brazil and other coffee-producing nations. Every country depends on other countries of the world to provide goods it needs. Each country also needs other countries to buy the goods it produces.

The Legend of Saint Ursula was painted between 1490 and 1495 by Vittore Carpaccio. Ten beautiful ships in the painting reflect the importance of that mode of transportation during that time. In the 1400s and 1500s, Europeans traveled by ship to the East to buy the silks and spices that they needed.

International trade makes it possible for the people of each country to have more of what they want and need. They can **import**, or bring in, goods they cannot produce efficiently. They can **export,** or send out, goods they can produce well. Sometimes a country imposes a **trade barrier** on imports or exports. A trade barrier limits the amount of a particular product that can be imported. Or it taxes that product. A trade barrier may make a product more scarce or more expensive. A country may impose a trade barrier to protect its own industries. For example, a country that makes automobiles may put up a trade barrier on cars imported from other countries.

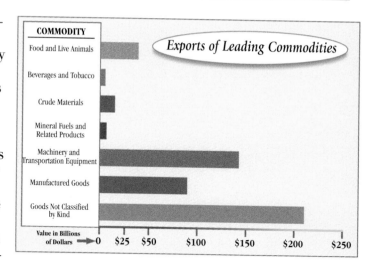

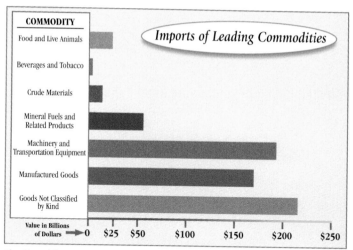

The United States exports and imports billions of dollars worth of goods. (Information provided by *Encyclopedia Brittanica.*)

Today, both transportation and communication keep becoming faster and faster. It is easier and easier to connect people and goods across the globe. As trade increases, the world's countries become more **interdependent**: They rely on each other for many things.

Culture

When you wake up each morning, you probably don't think twice about eating your breakfast cereal, putting on blue jeans, and going to school in a large brick building. But if you visited a country in Africa or Asia, you would find that people do some of these things very differently. All these aspects of your life are a result of your culture. **Culture** is the entire way of life shared by a group of people. It includes language, food, housing, ceremonies, and customs. A part of a population that has ancestry and culture in common is called an **ethnic group**.

Culture includes language, ceremonies, customs, and manner of dress. This woman of the Masai people of Africa wears the traditional dress of that group.

Language is an important aspect of culture. People in every culture use language to communicate. About 3,000 languages are spoken today. The kinds of food people eat, how they eat, and when they eat are also elements of culture. For example, people in many parts of Africa eat only one main meal every

Typical regional clothing of Rajasthan, India.

day. In many societies, males and females generally eat separately. Environmental factors also influence many aspects of culture. For example, people who live in tropical areas may wear one or two pieces of cloth draped around their body. People who live in colder climates need to wear warmer clothing.

Religion is a very important aspect of culture. Often,

most of the people in a geographical area may practice the same religion. For example, Christianity is the major religion in North America, while Islam is the major religion in northern Africa and the Middle East. Religion affects not only people's beliefs but many of their customs.

The culture of a people can change over time. Sometimes changes in science and technology bring changes in culture. When different cultures come into contact, both may be affected. People from one culture might want to adopt some customs of the other. This can cause conflict within a society between those who want to change and those who do not.

World Regions

Culture is one way to define **regions** of the world. A region is an area with one or more common features. Geographers use regions to help them study world patterns. There are many ways to define a region. A geographer might divide the world into regions based on climate or soils. When the post office divided the United States into zip codes, it was creating a kind of region to help make its job easier. Regions are a very useful idea that helps people learn about the world or do their jobs.

When geographers define a region, they consider culture, physical environment, and people's history. Within each geographic region, the people share some aspects of their culture and have some shared history. Sometimes there are disagreements about the exact boundaries of a region.

Canada and the United States are considered one region. The two countries have many aspects of culture in common: ancestry, language, housing, food, and customs. Mexico is also in the continent of North America, but it is not considered part of the same region. That's because Mexico is different from the United States and Canada in important ways. Mexico has more in common with the countries of Central America and South America. Mexico, Central America, and South America are considered a region: Latin America. They share elements of culture, language, and history.

United States and Canada

The North American countries of Canada and the United States have many similarities. They are both wealthy nations. The wealth comes in part from their rich natural resources and farm lands. Both countries were colonized in the 1600s by the English and French, so many aspects of their cultures are similar. Both countries have excellent school systems for their citizens. Both have many museums and libraries.

Canadians and Americans have similar diets. People in both countries eat plenty of beef, pork, and chicken and a wide variety of vegetables. Many citizens of both countries can afford to eat out at restaurants often and have much leisure time. One popular activity is playing and watching sports. In the United States, baseball, football, and basketball are popular. In Canada, hockey is the most popular sport.

There are differences between the two nations. Immigrants from many parts of the world have had a great effect on the cultures of both the United States and Canada. But people from different parts of the world have brought different aspects of their cultures to their new countries. For example, African Americans developed jazz music and other art forms in the United States. Hispanic Americans have added many interesting foods and

At 3,851,809 square miles (10, 014,703 square kilometers), Canada is the largest country in North America.

architectural styles to United States culture. Canada has been influenced by immigrants from other cultures. Right now, Canada receives a large number of immigrants from Asia.

Canada and the United States are the largest countries in North America. They also make up a large **culture region**. A culture region is an area in which the people share ways of life that are more alike than different. The people in a culture region often have similar customs, languages, religions, history, and economic development. Both the United States and Canada have a British heritage. English is a dominant language in both countries. Canada actually has two official languages— English and French. One of Canada's provinces, Quebec, is mainly French-speaking. Both countries have advanced technology and developed economies.

Latin America

The region of Latin America includes South America, Mexico, Central America, and the islands of the West Indies. Latin America has people of many ethnic backgrounds. The original inhabitants were American Indians. These people had been in the area since about 6000 B.C. Europeans settled here in

the late 1400s. They brought African slaves with them. The people of Latin America are mostly whites, blacks, Indians, and those of mixed Indian and white descent or of mixed black and white descent. Most Latin Americans are Christians. Most of these are Roman Catholics.

Nearly two thirds of Latin Americans speak Spanish. About one third speak Portuguese. Portuguese is Brazil's official language. Small numbers of people speak French, Dutch, English, or a traditional Indian language. Seventy percent of Latin Americans live in cities. In most countries, more and

Rio de Janeiro shows the gap between rich and poor.

more people in the cities can afford good housing, a car, and good clothing. But many urban residents still live in poor slums. The 30 percent who live in rural areas have a poorer standard of living than the urban middle class. Many work for poor wages on sugar, banana, coffee, or cotton plantations.

In many Latin American nations the governments are working to improve education. However, some poorer countries have a **literacy rate** of less than 50 percent. The literacy rate is the percentage of people over 15 who can read. Many areas cannot afford enough schools for their populations. In addition, many poor students must leave school to earn money.

Latin America is famous for its festive carnivals. Carnival time is especially spectacular in Rio de Janeiro.

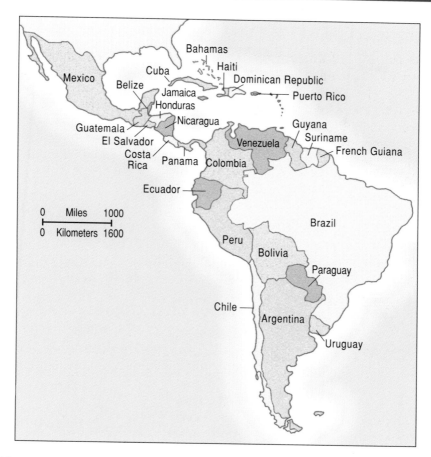

Many Latin American nations have rich mineral resources. The economies of most of the nations have relied on exporting these mineral resources and farm products. More and more, the nations are building factories. As this happens, more people are moving from rural areas to the cities, looking for work.

In Latin America, city populations are growing rapidly. The cities are struggling to meet the housing needs of the people. They are working to provide electricity, water, sewers, and roadways. But the cities cannot keep up with the rapid growth. As a result, many people live in poor conditions. The nations of Latin America face the challenge of growth. They are working to meet the needs of their people and to become industrial nations.

Europe

Europe is a mixture of the old and the new. It has been civilized since the time of ancient Greece, beginning in 3000 B.C. In the 1700s, Europe started the Industrial Revolution (see page 72–73). Even today, reminders of Europe's ancient beginnings stand alongside modern factories. The ancient Colosseum in Rome is in the middle of a busy modern city.

Europe is a continent connected to the Asian continent. It includes part of Russia, the largest country in the world, on the east. About one eighth of the world's population lives in Europe. Together, Europe and Asia are the most densely populated landmass in the world. Many different ethnic groups live in Europe.

Many differences exist in Europe between the north and south, the east and the west, and the rural and urban areas. Northern Europe contains more industry. The south has more farms.

For many years, Western Europe enjoyed more political and economic freedom than Eastern Europe. During those years, Communist governments in some eastern nations strictly regulated people's lives. From 1989 to 1991, these governments fell. Now these countries are working to develop industries and their economies.

The countries of Europe are very diverse. Each has its own history, language, customs, government, and economy. Even regions within a country may differ vastly from one another. For example, northern Italy has more factories and cities than southern Italy. Yet, the countries of Europe are working to cooperate with one another. They have

A street vendor sells homemade shoes in the heart of Moscow, Russia. Russia is the largest country in the world.

formed the European Union. The Union is an organization of Western European countries that work together in such areas as economic development, security, justice, and foreign policy. It has grown from an earlier organization called the European Economic Community. Members of the European Union include both large and small nations. Some members are the United Kingdom, France, Italy, and Germany. Smaller countries that belong include Belgium and Luxembourg.

Member nations work together to encourage economic growth and development. The nations have adopted common policies and rules in transportation, agriculture, health, immigration, and safety.

Africa

Africa is the second largest continent in area. One eighth of the earth's people live there. Two thirds of Africans live in rural areas. Africa's economy is the least developed of any populated continent.

Many people in Africa speak Arabic or Swahili. However, more than 1,000 languages are spoken in Africa. Most ethnic groups have their own language. Many educated Africans speak English, French, or Portuguese as well as their ethnic language. European languages were brought to Africa when European countries colonized the continent in the 1800s.

The culture of countries in northern Africa differs from the culture of the countries south of the Sahara. Most of the people in the north are Arabs and follow the Islam religion. (Followers of the Islam religion are called Muslims.) About half the people in these countries live in rural areas. They raise livestock or grow crops. These people

Most of the people in northern Africa follow the Islam religion. This Muslim place of worship, called a **mosque**, is located in Cairo, Egypt.

often live in houses with mud walls that keep out heat. They rarely leave their villages. Life in a city is more like modern American life. But many cities are crowded and have problems with electricity and water.

Most people south of the Sahara are black Africans. Seventy-five percent of them live in rural areas. In Nigeria, in west Africa, people in rural areas live in houses made of grass, dried wood, or mud. The houses are grouped together in compounds within villages. As in northern Africa, many people in southern Africa are moving to big cities. These cities have a more modern lifestyle, but they also have problems with overcrowding.

Most African nations only gained their independence from European rule after 1960. When Europeans colonized Africa, they sometimes drew borders that separated a single ethnic group into different countries or placed ethnic groups that were enemies in the same country. This caused problems between the countries. It also created problems within countries. When the African nations gained independence, many had weak or harsh governments. People became unhappy with their governments. Some were enemies with other ethnic groups within their countries. These problems have led to civil wars in many countries. A **civil war** is a war between groups inside a country.

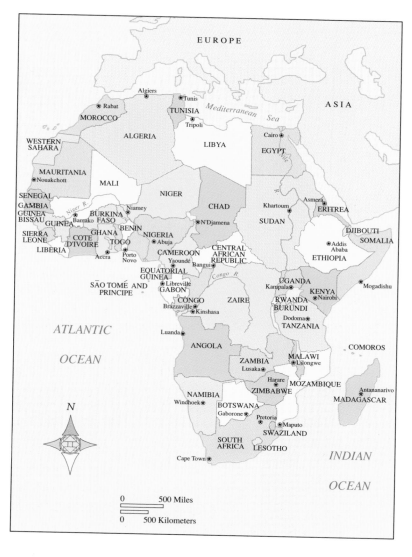

West Asia

West Asia was the birthplace of three of the world's main religions: Christianity, Islam, and Judaism. Except for two nations, most people in West Asian countries practice Islam. In Cyprus, Christianity is the main religion. Most people of Israel practice Judaism.

West Asia contains many of the countries often known as the Middle East. Although West Asia is covered with desert, about half of the region's people work on farms. Most of them do not own their own land. They rent land to grow barley, wheat, dates, or olives. They live in villages with dried mud houses. Men gather in a village's bathhouse or teahouse or mosque. A **mosque** is a Muslim place of worship.

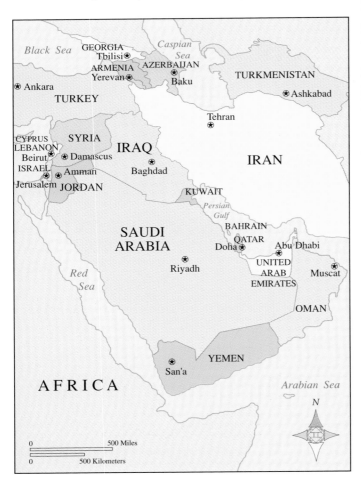

Another form of traditional rural life is that of the nomad. The Bedouins of Saudi Arabia are nomads. These herders travel through the deserts with their camels, sheep, or goats. They live in tents made of animal hides. Wherever they find water or grazing lands, the Bedouins set up their tents.

Nomads of the Shammar tribe of Saudia Arabia have a meal inside their large tent.

Islam has an important role in most countries of the Middle East. Some countries are ruled by religious leaders. Iran is one of these countries. Others have strict rules based on the Islam faith. Saudi Arabia has such rules. In several countries, Muslim women have been required to wear a long robe and a face-covering veil when they go out in public. They have not been allowed to drive a car or work with men. The Muslim governments recognize the rights of girls to get an education, but families often do not allow their daughters to go to school. This is especially true in rural areas. Some Muslim women are trying to gain more freedom.

Life in Israel differs in many ways from life in other West Asian countries. Israel was founded in 1948 as a home for Jews from all over the world. Ninety percent of Israelis live in cities.

The way of life in some West Asian countries has changed because of the oil industry. Many of the nations have vast oil reservoirs. Most of these countries are located on the Persian Gulf. They export the oil throughout the world. As a result, the nations have become very wealthy.

The oil industry is a major source of wealth around the Persian Gulf.

South Asia

Perhaps you have practiced the exercise called yoga. Maybe you have heard sitar music or have seen pictures of the Taj Mahal. These are all parts of the culture of India, the country that occupies three fourths of South Asia. Pakistan and Bangladesh are also part of South Asia. South Asia is separated from the rest of Asia by mountains and deserts. About one fifth of the world's people live in South Asia.

Most of the people of this region belong to one of two major religions: Hinduism and Islam. More than 95 percent of the people in Pakistan are Muslims, and Islam is the official religion of Bangladesh. In India, 83 percent of the people are Hindu. India is also home to many Christians, Buddhists, Muslims, and Sikhs.

Top: Children learn in an open-air school in the village of Dalbandin in Baluchistan, Pakistan.
Above: A village in Fatehabad in the northern state of Haryana in India flooded in 1993. These children take advantage of the situation to have a little fun in the flood waters with some friendly water buffalo.

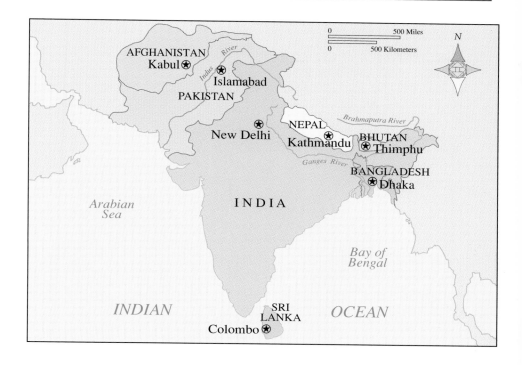

The chief language of India is Hindi. But 16 other major languages and 1,000 minor ones are also spoken. Indian states are organized so that they are populated by people who speak the same language. The Hindu religion plays a big role in people's lives. Each person in a Hindu family is born into a certain **caste**, or social group. Several thousand castes exist. A person's caste determines the jobs he or she will choose. It also determines who the person's friends will be. The caste system is traditional, but it is loosening up. The current government is against the system.

Less than 30 percent of the people in Pakistan, Bangladesh, and India live in cities. The cities in India are very crowded. Many people live behind and above the shops that line the streets. The streets are also full of homeless people because the country's population has grown rapidly, and there is much poverty. Many children must help support their families, so educating everyone is difficult. Literacy is increasing, though. About one third of the adults in the region can read and write.

East Asia

Like the rest of the Asian continent, East Asia is one of the most densely populated regions in the world. One quarter of all the people in the world live in East Asia. It includes China, Japan, North Korea, South Korea, and Taiwan. China is the country with the world's largest population.

The traditional religions of East Asia are Confucianism, Taoism, Shintoism, and Buddhism. These religions influence people's way of life. In East Asia, great importance is placed on respect for one's ancestors and on getting an education.

The two largest countries in East Asia, China and Japan, are very different from one another. China is one of the world's poorest nations. About three fourths of the people work on farms. A Communist government came into power in China in 1949. The new government improved rural life, but the rural standard of living is still low. Japan is wealthier and more modern than other countries in East Asia. About three

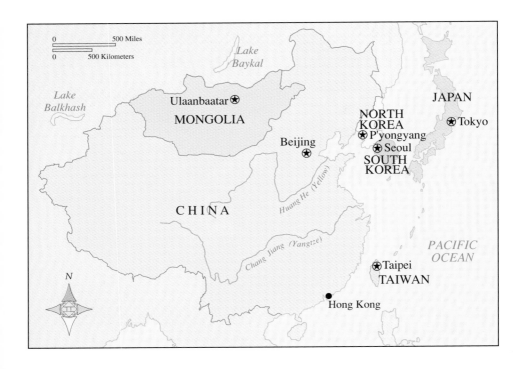

fourths of Japan's population lives in cities, and almost everyone can find a job. Japan has a very strong economy. It is one of the leading industrial nations of the world.

The economic situation could change. China's economy is developing very rapidly. China now exports many products to other nations. With its growing economy and huge population, China is one of the world's largest and most important economies. Taiwan and South Korea, too, have been developing industries and exporting goods.

In China, the Communists have tried to improve the country's education. Although 95 percent of Chinese children attend elementary school, most drop out of middle school. In Japan, students compete for good educations in the country's best schools. Even in grade school, students compete to get into the best schools and to be the best students.

Natural disasters are a serious problem in East Asia. It is a densely populated region located in an area that has many earthquakes and volcanoes. Flooding is

Top: Tokyo is the capital of Japan. *Above:* Bicycles are the major form of transportation in China.

another threat. Recently, a strong earthquake destroyed the city of Kobe, Japan. Some countries are working to protect their people from natural disasters. For example, in Japan, buildings are built so that they are less likely to topple during earthquakes.

Southeast Asia

Southeast Asia includes the countries of Brunei, Malaysia, Burma, Myanmar, Cambodia, Laos, Thailand, Vietnam, Singapore, Indonesia, and the Philippines. It has gone through many changes in the last 50 years. Most of these countries gained their independence from Europe after 1945. As the countries became independent, different groups fought to control the governments. The result was civil wars and uprisings in many nations. Recently, the governments have become more stable.

Most Southeast Asians are traditionally farmers. Here, a man dries rice near Ho Chi Minh City in Vietnam. Rice is the major crop of Southeast Asia.

The Southeast Asian countries have rich resources. These include minerals, forests, good fishing, and fertile soil. Most Southeast Asians are traditionally farmers. For thousands of years, they have lived in small villages and farmed. The major crop is rice.

Many countries in Southeast Asia have large populations for their size. But they have not had to import food. That's because the rice crops have been able to feed the people. The rice is cultivated during monsoon season, May to July. A **monsoon** is a strong storm that follows the dry season in South Asia and Southeast Asia. Monsoons bring heavy rains that flood the land. They make it possible to grow important crops. The lives of many people in Southeast Asia and South Asia depend on the monsoons.

Although farming is still a most important industry, more and more Southeast Asian countries are changing to an industrial economy. Lower-cost labor has led many international busi-

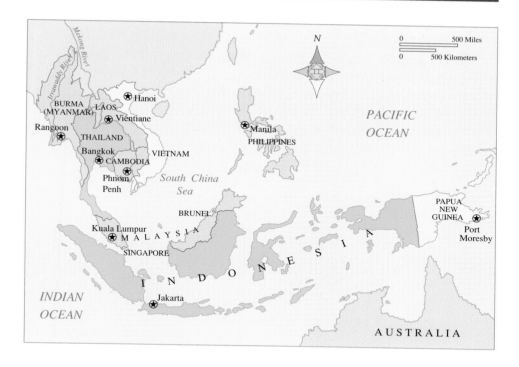

nesses to set up factories in Southeast Asia. Thailand is a good example of a country that is becoming more industrial. Thailand is working to build factories that use its many natural resources. For instance, the country is expanding its oil-refining industry.

The main religion of Thailand and other parts of Southeast Asia is Buddhism. It teaches that true peace is obtained by getting rid of desires for wealth. Young Buddhists are urged to become monks for at least a short time. About 40 percent of them do become monks. On the other hand, young people in Thailand are influenced by American and European lifestyles, too. And, Islam is another major religion in the region.

Other aspects of life remain traditional. Bicycles, not cars, are the main form of transportation. Houses are made of wood or thatch. They are built on stilts to prevent flooding near rivers and canals.

Oceania

Oceania is the name geographers give to a group of thousands of islands in the Pacific Ocean. The region includes small and large Pacific islands. New Guinea and New Zealand are part of Oceania. Although Australia is itself a continent, it is grouped geographically with these islands.

For a long time, Oceania was very diverse and cut off from the rest of the world. Today, good communication and transportation systems put most of the area in better touch with the rest of the world.

Most of the Pacific islands are small and have small populations. The people lead different ways of life. Some have been strongly influenced by European cultures. Others live in much the same way as their ancestors did. Still others combine traditional and more modern ways of life.

New Zealand and Australia were settled by the British in the 1700s. They became independent countries at the beginning of this century. They have modern economies, and most of

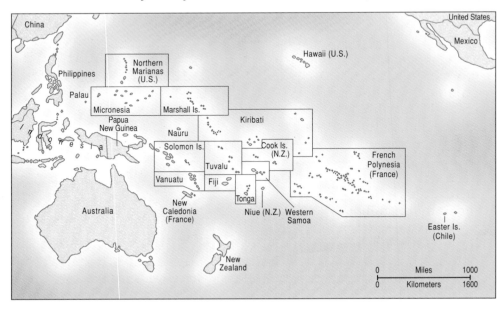

Oceania is known for its unique plant and animal life. This mother kangaroo and her cute baby live in Australia.

the people have European ancestors. Many other Oceanian islands were still colonies of European countries or the United States until the 1970s or later. These countries are still developing.

Agriculture is the largest economic activity in the area. But the countries export their crops to the world. You will probably find fruit produced in Oceania in your grocery store. In addition, mining, manufacturing, and tourism have become major industries.

Many Pacific Islanders and some Australians live in small rural communities and villages. More live in major towns and cities. More than four fifths of Australians live in cities and towns. Seventy percent of those people live in cities with more than 100,000 people.

Oceania's long isolation has resulted in a natural environment filled with unique plants and animals. This is the only place you can find kangaroos, wombats, koala bears, platypuses, dingoes, and Tasmanian devils. These interesting and unusual animals have helped the travel industry. Tourists and scientists come to see the animals in their natural habitats.

Australia is considered a part of Oceania, though it is also a continent.

Cultural Change

Do we live in a "world culture"? Some geographers think that everyone in the world is quickly becoming the same. We're wearing the same clothes, eating the same foods, and listening to the same music. These changes are made possible because of modern transportation and communication.

Contact between two cultures causes changes in both of them. Each culture borrows cultural traits that seem useful or interesting from the other. The process of a cultural trait spreading from its original society is called **diffusion**. For example, corn was a crop originally grown in North America. It quickly spread to Europe and then all around the world. Another example of cultural diffusion is jazz music. Jazz was first played in the southern United States in the late 1800s. The music spread around the world in the mid-twentieth century.

These children of Rwanda, Africa, wear Western-style clothing instead of their traditional attire. This is an example of **diffusion**.

The spread of jazz was due to radio, recordings, and international travel by jazz musicians.

Another cause of cultural change is **assimilation**. Assimilation happens when a person takes on the traits of a different culture. Some fear that their culture's distinctive traits are being lost as people adopt the traits of other cultures. For example,

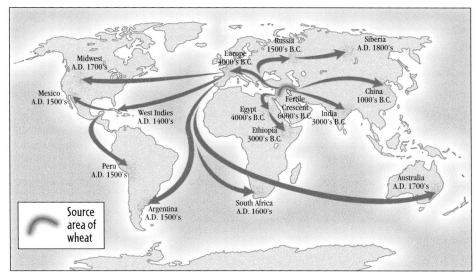

Wheat was a crop originally grown in the Fertile Crescent of the Middle East. It spread first to Europe and northern Africa, then eventually throughout the world.

people in France have used more and more American slang in recent years. Some French people have tried to stop the use of English words and phrases in France. They are afraid of losing the French language. Likewise, in parts of Asia, many people have left their traditional dress and values. They have adopted the clothing and values of Western countries. Other people in those societies are against these changes. This is especially true in Islamic countries.

A McDonald's restaurant opened in Beijing, China, in 1992. As China attracts more American businesses, the Chinese people may take on the traits of Western culture.

Interacting with the Environment

Modification and Adaptation

Humans must live in their environment on earth. Whether they live on the frigid Arctic tundra or in the tropical rain forest, people have a relationship with their natural surroundings. Geographers are very interested in how people interact with their environment. We interact with the environment in two ways: by **adaptation** and by **modification**.

People **adapt** to their environment in many ways. That is, they change their habits to make it easier to live in their surroundings. In cold climates, people build houses that keep out the frigid weather. They also wear clothes that keep them warm. For example, the Inuit

The Inuit people of the Arctic have adapted to their harsh environment.

people of Arctic areas built sod or snow houses with thick walls to protect them from the snow and cold, and they made warm clothing from animal skins.

When we use electric air conditioning to cool the air, we are **modifying**, or changing, the environment. Farmers modify their environment by irrigating their land, fertilizing the soil, and planting certain crops. Using chemicals to kill insects is also a form of environmental modification. When workers clear a natural wooded area, they are modifying the environment. When miners take coal or other minerals from the earth, they are changing the environment. When people create industries or drive cars, the pollutants they create can change the environment.

Modification can have both good and bad results. The modifications farmers make to produce crops help feed earth's population. The modifications brought about by pollution cause dangers to humans and animals alike. Building a dam on a river can have both good and bad results. The dam might provide electricity for millions of people. It could also endanger the survival of plants and animals that rely on the river for food.

A dam is a form of environmental modification. This is the Roosevelt Dam on the Salt River in Arizona. The lake behind the dam is called Roosevelt Lake.

Natural Resources

We enjoy the things the earth offers every day. Sunshine, trees, and cool water give us pleasure. More important, they are necessary to life. These parts of nature and many others are our **natural resources**. Earth's natural resources include air, plants and animals, iron, and petroleum. Natural resources can be renewable or nonrenewable.

A **renewable** resource can be replaced after it has been used. Renewable resources include sunlight, air, and water. These resources are necessary to life for people and all living things. Soil, trees and other plants, and animals are also renewable resources. Soil is essential for growing crops for foods. Plants and animals provide food and other products such as medicines.

Earth contains an abundance of all these resources. Some renewable resources are limitless. Sunlight is a good example of this kind of resource. But others must be conserved properly. If the air is polluted by chemicals from factories and cars, plant and animal life will be harmed. If forests are destroyed carelessly, other plant and animal life can suffer or

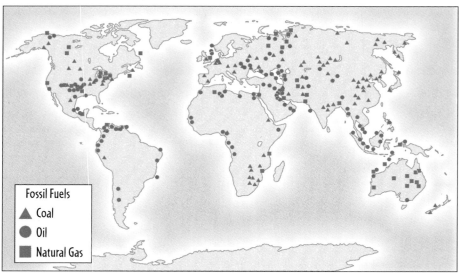

This map shows the location of fossil fuels around the world.

Lettuce is an example of a renewable resource because more lettuce can be grown after this has been used.

die out. If farmers misuse soil, it can take hundreds of years to replace. Unless these renewable resources are conserved carefully, they will be used up faster than earth's natural processes can replace them.

A **nonrenewable** resource cannot be replaced once it is used up. Minerals are one kind of nonrenewable resource. They take thousands or millions of years to form. Right now, they are being taken out of the earth faster than they are forming. Fortunately, some of these resources are **recyclable**. After they have been used for one product, they can be processed and used again. Copper and aluminum are often recycled. Other resources, such as iron, are mined but are stored for later use. Another kind of nonrenewable resource is fossil fuel: coal, oil, and natural gas.

The countries of the world have different natural resources. They extract them from the earth and use them differently, too. Often, the wealthiest countries are those with rich natural resources. For example, the United States and Canada have abundant natural resources. They have used these resources to provide many comforts for their citizens. In other places, this is not always the case. Many countries in Southeast Asia have rich mineral resources. They are beginning to develop these more, so that their people can enjoy a higher standard of living. Countries that do not have important natural resources must buy them from other countries.

Oil is a fossil fuel, which is a nonrenewable source.

Energy Resources

Did you know that the energy used to heat and light your home may have come from plants and animals that died millions of years ago? **Fossil fuels** come from the remains of plants and animals that died long ago. Coal, oil, and natural gas are fossil fuels. When the organisms died, they were buried by layers of rock and soil. Gradually, they turned into substances we use for fuel. Fossil fuels provide three quarters of the world's energy. Energy is needed for everyday life in the home and office, industry, and transportation.

The world has enough coal to use for several hundred years. Unfortunately, using coal releases large amounts of pollutants into the air. Also, coal mining can damage the land. For these reasons, oil and gas are preferred fuels for heating and transportation. Oil and gas are also easier to transport than coal. However, the known reserves of oil and gas are getting smaller. They will last for only one or two more centuries. In addition, oil and gas also release harmful pollutants into the air.

Because fossil fuels are polluting and nonrenewable, scientists are exploring many other energy sources. **Wind energy** has been used for thousands of years to power sailing ships

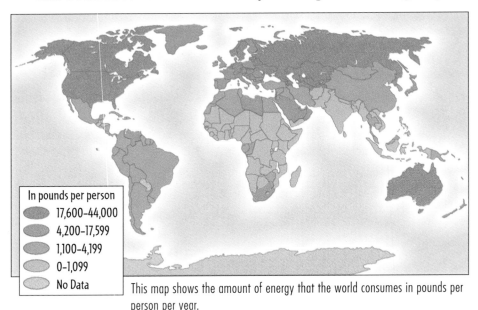

In pounds per person
- 17,600–44,000
- 4,200–17,599
- 1,100–4,199
- 0–1,099
- No Data

This map shows the amount of energy that the world consumes in pounds per person per year.

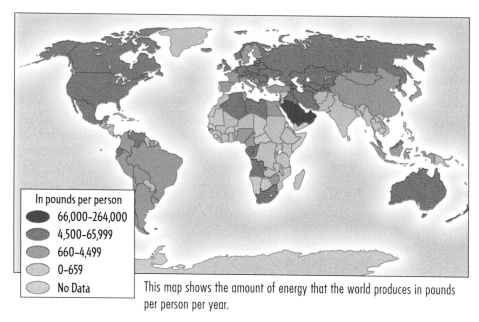

In pounds per person
- 66,000–264,000
- 4,500–65,999
- 660–4,499
- 0–659
- No Data

This map shows the amount of energy that the world produces in pounds per person per year.

and windmills. Today, wind turbines (engines) provide power in places where the wind blows fairly regularly. **Geothermal energy** is another kind of energy. It can be used in places where hot water deep in the earth is released through springs. **Hydroelectric power** plants are housed in dams on rivers or other water sources. They provide power from moving water. **Nuclear energy** is released by splitting the nucleus of an atom. It can provide huge amounts of power. All these alternative energy sources have their advantages and disadvantages. For example, nuclear power plants create dangerous radioactive wastes. Getting energy from sunlight and wind can cost a lot of money. Scientists are working to improve the technology for making alternative energy sources more usable for everyone.

This nuclear power plant produces a huge amount of power. Unfortunately, nuclear power plants create dangerous radioactive wastes.

Environmental Pollution

If you have ever flown near a big city in an airplane, you may have seen a dark haze hanging over the city's skyline. If you live near a factory, you may have smelled fumes or seen smoke produced by industry. If you live near a river or lake, you may have seen water dirtied by an oil slick or garbage. All of these are forms of **pollution**: releasing harmful materials into the environment.

The effects of **air pollution** show up in stone buildings in large cities. Polluted air blackens the stone and eats away at it. If dirty air can damage buildings, imagine what it does to people! Burning eyes, headaches, and lung diseases such as asthma and lung cancer can be caused or worsened by air pollution. Air pollution is caused mainly by burning fossil fuels to power cars, trucks, and factories. Burning gasoline produces dangerous amounts of pollutants. When they mix with moisture in the air, these chemicals cause acid rain. Acid rain can damage forests and bodies of water far from the source of the pollution.

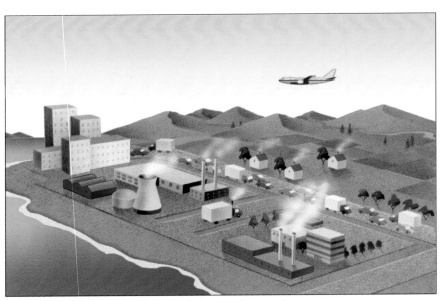

How many causes of air pollution can you find in this illustration?

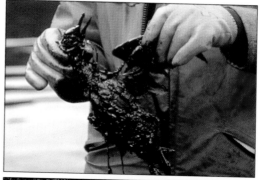

One dangerous result of air pollution has been the thinning of the earth's **ozone layer.** This protective layer in earth's atmosphere keeps out the sun's harmful ultraviolet rays. These rays can cause skin cancer in people and also harm other living things. Chemicals used in aerosol sprays, refrigeration, and foam products are destroying the ozone layer. Chemicals released by burning fossil fuels also trap heat in the earth's atmosphere. Scientists believe this could cause global warming that would affect ecosystems all over the world.

Not only the air but the water and the land are being polluted. Sources of the pollution are hazardous wastes from industries, solid garbage, and pesticides. Polluted water has far-reaching effects. Eating fish that have consumed chemicals such as pesticides may be harmful to people.

Top: The oil tanker *Exxon Valdez* spilled millions of gallons of oil along the coast of Alaska in 1989, polluting the water and destroying many birds. *Bottom:* Other results of water pollution include dead fish and destroyed marshlands.

Fortunately, the problem of pollution is recognized worldwide. People are trying to reduce pollution from vehicles and industry. However, everyone needs to contribute to the effort to keep the earth clean.

Conservation

In the past, people have taken natural resources for granted. They thought clean water, healthy forests, and fertile soil would always exist. Since the Industrial Revolution, there are many more people in the world. More people consume more natural resources. We now realize that earth's resources must be carefully cared for. The careful use of natural resources is called **conservation**.

Scientists have learned that the earth's ecosystems are closely connected. If a forest is destroyed, many other plants and animals lose their habitats. Their existence is threatened. Also, destroying forests causes imbalances in the amounts of oxygen and carbon dioxide in the air.

People now realize that they must plan carefully in clearing forests to make way for farmland or buildings. However, it's not always easy to control the clearing of land for farming. In some parts of the world, people need new farmland to feed

This chart indicates how long our fossil fuels and some natural resources will last at current rates of usage. By the year 2300, everything will be depleted unless we find alternatives or learn to conserve.

Some cities and towns provide recycling bins in neighborhood parking lots.

themselves and their families. The challenge is to find ways to produce more food and improve people's lives while protecting the environment and natural resources. Governments and people all over the world are working toward this goal.

Forests are one natural resource that people are trying to conserve. Another is soil. Soil loses its nutrients when farmers plant the same crop over and over again. Water and wind erode soil when it is plowed carelessly. Another dangerous practice is **clear-cutting** of trees: cutting down all the trees in a large area. Clear-cutting increases soil erosion. Since soil is needed for growing the food people need, farmers and builders must help conserve it.

Fossil fuels burned for energy are being used up fast. In addition, these fuels cause air pollution that harms people and other living things. While scientists look for new, clean energy sources, people must conserve the fuel they use.

Animals and fish are also natural resources that people must conserve. Many kinds of animals have become extinct because they have been hunted carelessly.

Everyone must help conserve earth's resources. How can you help? Recycling newspapers helps save forests. Recycling aluminum cans and automobiles helps conserve minerals. Cutting down on car and electricity use cleans the air and conserves fossil fuels. Cutting down on water use conserves the supply of freshwater.

Recycling everything from aluminum cans to automobiles will help conserve earth's resources. Please do your part.

Natural Hazards

Suppose you are sleeping in your bed and your whole house begins to shake. Or imagine you are walking to the town market when hot volcanic lava flows down a hillside. What if you are playing outside when a huge swirling wind appears on the horizon? Everyone has seen some of nature's dangerous surprises in movies and on television. Earthquakes, volcanoes, and tornadoes are scary even when you are watching them on a screen. To people in various parts of the world, these emergencies are very real. Adapting to our environment includes responding to natural hazards.

An **earthquake** is a sudden shaking in the earth. It is caused by energy released by shifting rock. Geologists have a theory called **plate tectonics**. According to the theory, earth's surface is made up of seven large plates and many smaller ones. These huge pieces are constantly shifting. Most earthquakes occur near a **fault**: the place where two plates come together. As the plates push or grind against each other, energy is stored inside the earth's crust. When the energy stored inside the rock becomes too great, the rock shifts, causing an earthquake.

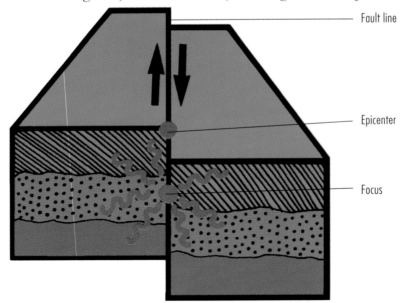

Fault line

Epicenter

Focus

This is an illustration of an earthquake. The break below the surface is the **focus**, and the point on earth's surface where the quake is felt is the **epicenter**.

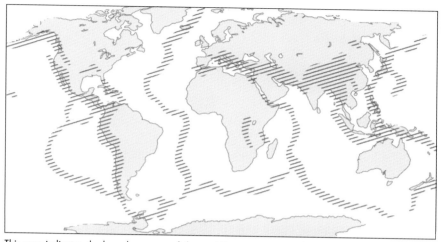

This map indicates the boundary areas of the world's major tectonic plates. Major earthquakes tend to occur along the red lines, though quakes can occur anywhere.

In a strong earthquake, much damage can occur. Buildings and roads can collapse. Water pipes can break. Electric wires and gas mains can break, causing fires. Earthquakes can also cause powerful ocean waves called **tsunami**.

The places that most often suffer earthquake damage are located near faults. One famous fault is the San Andreas Fault in California. On the other side of the Pacific, many earthquakes also happen in Japan. In fact, there are faults all along the edges of the Pacific Ocean. Near these faults there are more earthquakes, and also more volcanoes, than in other parts of the world. That's why these fault zones are known as the Ring of Fire.

The scientists who study earthquakes are called **seismologists**. They have invented instruments to measure earthquakes and learned much about how they happen. But it is still not possible to predict earthquakes or to prevent them. People who live near faults must adapt to their environment. In fault areas, buildings are built to withstand the strong shaking of earthquakes. People learn about the best ways to stay safe when an earthquake hits.

Tectonic plates are also responsible for another kind of natural hazard, a **volcano**. Volcanoes are formed by eruptions of molten rock from beneath earth's surface. When a volcano erupts, ashes, lava, hot gases, and rock fragments come out. Like earthquakes, volcanoes usually occur near places where tectonic plates meet.

Most volcanoes are located along a belt around the Pacific Ocean. Some volcanoes erupt constantly and are called **active volcanoes.** **Dormant volcanoes** have

A volcano erupts in Hawaii, spewing lava and hot gases into the sky.

been inactive for a while but may erupt again. **Extinct volcanoes** have not erupted in recorded history and probably will not erupt again. The lava, gases, and rocks from an erupting volcano can be extremely destructive. When Mount St. Helens in Washington erupted in 1980, 60 people were killed. Many trees, houses, and roads were destroyed.

Other types of natural hazards are related to the weather. Floods, hurricanes, and tornadoes are examples of this kind

of hazard. A **flood** happens when water overflows onto land that is normally dry. A flood may be caused by heavy rains, melting snows, or hurricanes. If several inches of rain fall in a short period, water can overflow the banks of streams and rivers and cause a flash flood. Because a flash flood is sudden and unexpected, it can cause death and destroy property.

Heavy summer rains caused this mighty river to overflow its banks. Floods can cause major damage to towns located near rivers and creeks.

People can prevent floods by controlling bodies of water. For example, they can build levees to hold back water. Or they can deepen channels in rivers so they do not overflow onto land. Conserving soil and forests is also helpful. It helps prevent too much water from running off the land into streams.

Tropical storms are another weather-related hazard. These storms form over warm ocean waters. They are called hurricanes, cyclones, or typhoons. A tropical storm brings huge amounts of rain as it travels from water onto land. It can also cause enormous, damaging waves. Tropical storms can bring floods to coastal areas.

A **tornado** is a dangerous storm that starts on land. It is a powerful, twisting column of air that can touch ground during a thunderstorm. A tornado is more powerful than any other kind of storm. It can lift cars and buildings in its path. The United States has more tornadoes than any other place on earth. Fortunately, weather forecasters are often able to predict tornadoes. They can warn people to seek shelter.

Natural disasters are a part of our environment that we cannot modify. But we can adapt to them. Learning more about earthquakes, volcanoes, floods, and storms is our best defense against these hazards.

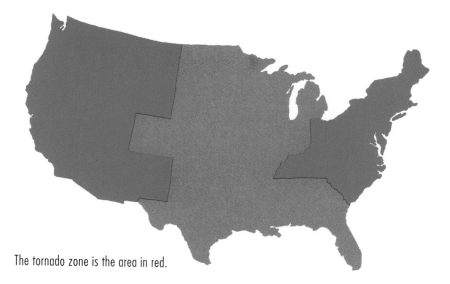

The tornado zone is the area in red.

Geography Is ...

Faraway places? Maps and globes? The Aborigines of Australia or the Zen Buddhists of Southeast Asia?

You have seen that geography is all this and more. The student of geography discovers the magnificent plant life of the tropical rain forest and the nomads who wander the barren deserts of Saudi Arabia. A geographer may study the GDP of developing countries and the population densities of the 50 states. Geographers are interested in the deepest

part of the ocean and the highest mountain on the earth. They want to know about the oxcarts of Thailand and the space shuttles of the United States.

When you study geography you may find you have much in common with people who seem to live a very different kind of life. You might try harder to conserve the earth's resources. You might develop a new fascination for the plants, birds, and animals of the world.

If you are interested in the world outside your front door, you are interested in geography. Perhaps you have found that learning about geography helps you learn about yourself.

Index